Overflowing Love

JOSEPH HARRIS

Overflowing Love

Copyright © 2019 Joseph Harris

Published by Destiny House Publishing, LLC.

All scripture verses quoted are from the KJV unless otherwise indicated.

No part of this document may be reproduced or transmitted in any form or by any means, electronic, mechanical, photocopying, recording, or otherwise, without prior written permission. Requests for permission to make copies of any part of the work should be submitted to:

Destiny House Publishing, LLC.

P.O. Box 19774

Detroit, MI 48219

www.destinyhousepublishing.com

inquiry@destinyhousepublishing.com

All rights reserved.

ISBN-13: 978-1-936867-46-2

DEDICATION

This book is dedicated first and foremost to my Lord, Jesus Christ and my parents, Joe Arthur Doyle and Gussie Doyle that gave me unconditional love. They were responsible for my life and all the success I have ever had. Jesus gets all the glory and thanksgiving. I am thankful for His love overflowing in my life by giving me great parents and a hero as a father. They both bless my life. Thanksgiving and glory to His name.

CONTENTS

Chapter		Page
1	Pray to Conceive & Give Birth	1
2	Love Intervention & Restore	56
3	Spiritual Momentum	73
4	Unequally Yoked	93
5	Love Fills Gaps	117

CHAPTER 1

PRAY TO CONCEIVE AND GIVE BIRTH

LOVE CODE

1 Samuel 1:15-20 And Hannah answered and said, No, my lord, I am a woman of a sorrowful spirit: I have drunk neither wine nor strong drink, but have poured out my soul before the Lord. Count not thine handmaid for a daughter of Belial: for out of the abundance of my complaint and grief have I spoken hitherto. Then Eli answered and said, Go in peace: and the God of Israel grant thee thy petition that thou hast asked of him. And she said, Let thine handmaid find grace in thy sight. So the woman went her way, and did eat, and her countenance was no more sad. And they rose up in the morning early, and worshipped before the Lord, and returned, and came to their house to Ramah: and Elkanah knew Hannah his wife; and the Lord remembered her. Wherefore it came to pass, when the time was come about after Hannah had conceived, that she bare a son, and called his name Samuel, saying, Because I have asked him of the Lord.

Every person has been birthed and nursed to life by a mother. Therefore, we see that God's power works on the inside, making it possible for a mother to conceive and give birth. This very thought should ignite a relationship with God for every woman alive. At the forefront of my thoughts, when it comes to mothers giving birth, besides Hannah: there was Mary, the mother of Jesus, and Elizabeth, the mother of John the Baptist. These two women also had a heart to give birth because God had ordained these moments in Joseph and Mary's life. Mary was a virgin and the mother of Jesus. She was told by Gabriel, the angel of God. He was sent to announce the virgin birth of a new King to be born in Bethlehem (Luke 1:26-38). This is one of God's greatest events on earth.

The love of Jesus Christ saved the entire world. From-birth to the cross and from the cross (John 19) to the grave demonstrates the power of the resurrection (Mark 16:9). God is always in the business of making His love overflow in our lives. I love Mark 16:9 because in it, Jesus' resurrection is revealed to a woman first. Her name was Mary Magdalene. Jesus had cast seven devils out of her.

After conception and the birth, a mother is there to nurture and help guide her child's life for success to receive blessings of the

Lord. God put us here to produce through the power of love. Nevertheless, when it comes to a child, God starts and finishes the process. God is in the life-giving business. He presents a new born baby as His master piece. You and I start off as a seed planted into our mother's womb, which came from our father. Please recognize that God is the leading factor in the creative process, including your birth and growth.

In this passage, God uses a Godly man to pronounce the birth of Samuel. It is powerful that God heard the words of Eli saying, "The God of Israel grant your request." Eli was speaking to God regarding Hannah's request that she might receive what she requested. This is powerful because Eli already knew by faith that God would grant the blessing of a baby to Hannah. The miracle of the story is God granted Hannah the power to conceive from the seed of Elkannah even when her womb was dead. It's a miracle that God caused a dead womb to produce life. It was Hannah's heartfelt prayer that God heard. I believe God moves on our behalf when there is a heartfelt prayer because only He knows the sincerity and love inside. God answers yes or no according to His will and purpose. It is still up to Him, no matter what the situation is at hand.

The word conceive means to become pregnant. Conception means the action of conceiving a child. Conception happens when

God says so, regardless of any condition that exists beforehand. God can deliver a child through a fertilized womb, that was once dead. There are various couples that have experienced the miraculous conception after the enemy tried to stop it. This simply means that God can give a woman a baby even when she least expects it. This passage is for every man and woman to believe and have hope that God can do the impossible. Luke 1:36-38 tells us "nothing is impossible for God." He is a miracle working God. Nevertheless, He wants us to make our requests known, because it proves to Him that we believe in Him and trust Him. Three of our greatest advantages in this life is the power to believe, the response to love God, and the choice to walk in obedience. Keep in mind, God's response depends on God's decision. He makes the final decision regardless of what we think or feel!

You and I, literally, owe our father and mother the highest respect and honor (Ephesians 6). Both parents must adhere to His word that says, "Train up a child in the way they shall go." In the scientific and psychological world, there is the nature vs nurture study. What is the most effective influence on a person, experiences or the environment?

One of the most powerful things that I have seen is a mother's love for her child. I call it a mother's love code activated. You can't miss a mother's love code for her children. The first thing is her power to love and nurse her newborn baby. It's placed inside of her body and spirit by God! She instinctively gives birth and nurtures her babies and all the other children. She knows each child and all about them. The second most powerful love code is her protection of her babies. It's built in her instincts to nurture and protect her babies. She will fight to the end for her babies. Many mothers may not be fully aware of the power inside them. At some point in that delivery room while she waits to give birth, the love of Jesus must enter her mind. After all, she is about to have an experience of a lifetime.

Mothers have what I call a birth and love code inside of her that consists of nurturing power. Her ability to nurture has so much power that it transfers into protection like a lioness or mother bear protecting her young cubs in the wild. She will go up against any force to protect her children. She was created with a lifetime of nurturing power. This nurturing power is instinctive within her. A mother has the potential to protect her off-springs. She will fight to the end. It is inside of her heart. Men must understand this blessing within her. Let her work it out in her life because it is from God. An example of a mother who nurtures is even in her fight for the life of her children. An example, a mother can lift an iron gate or small car from her child's foot or body; she can suddenly get the strength to pick up and move that heavy load. In another instance, a mother would be willing to fight a bear or lion to save her child's life. You see everything is already built inside of her. Her instincts will surprise any threat. I watched a movie where a mother's instinct was so strong that she was able to discern who the man was that backed his car over her and almost killed her child.

A MOTHER'S HEART TO BIRTH

The love a mother has for her children is a blessing. She stays in the ready position to guard her children. Her instincts are perfect and aligned. I'm speaking of a true mother. A mother's heart is with her children. You can see it with humans and in animal life. If you are not careful, you would think that she worships her children. I am sure there are some cases in which mothers are worshipping their children. But I am sure they are not doing it intentionally. A mother's instincts are powerful. It's powerful because she not only has a love code for her child, she also has a love code for her husband. Read the story of Hannah regarding her request for a baby and you will understand the power of giving the child back to God. If you are a mother, you should want the best for your children by giving them back to God for service (1 Samuel 1:16-19). Don't hesitate because in the Old Testament,

Moses and Joshua taught that parents are to teach their children about God.

God blessed Hannah! Hannah's son, Samuel, the prophet ended up in the book of Hebrews, listed in the Hall of Faith book (Hebrews 11:32). This Samuel was a judge and the prophet that God sent to anoint King Saul who was known as the first king of Israel. He also anointed King David the next king of Israel. He poured the oil and the anointing of the Lord came over him. It is so powerful because the Prophet Samuel's name means (in Hebrew) God heard. God heard his mother Hannah and the priest Eli. God also used the Prophet Samuel as a man that hears from God. It's also powerful because it seems that Samuel always delivered a message from God that involved God's instructions on destroying and birthing. The key to Samuel's deliverance was obedience in every way. Samuel was in tuned with the voice of the Lord. He could hear from God.

Perhaps the peak of these blessing takes us to the fact that Hannah gave Samuel back to the Lord. She kept her word because she knew in her heart to put God first. God always comes first in the heart and service of His people. Another mother that was successful in the Bible was Moses' mother. She took a chance at saving his life by placing baby Moses in the Nile River to keep Pharaoh's soldiers from killing him. Pharaoh had ordered that all male babies be drowned. But Moses' mother placed him in God's hand. After living in the Pharaoh's Egyptian palace and breaking away, later Moses became God's deliverer. He delivered God's people out of the hands of Pharaoh. Moses' mother's name was Jochebed (Exodus 2:1). If you want to be a success in life when it comes to your children, pray to the Lord and give them over to Him. Take them to the priest and get them dedicated and baptized. Help them to understand how to give their lives to God (Romans 10:9). You can do it! See 1 Samuel 1 and Luke 2 regarding the child God gave you.

It took a while for me to understand that the nurturing power of love is built inside of a mother. She has a personal Godly designed nurturing code for her babies. Her nurturing power as a mother makes her a giver to the point that her love overflows. God put a nurturing spirit inside of the mother and it can get stronger and stronger each time, she gives birth to another child. Psychologist calls it nature versus nurture to some degree.

GROW UP AND LEAVE THE NEST

LET GO, LET GOD!

On another level, my mother knew when to help her kids grow up and when to push them out of the nest. Mother eagles feed and nourish their babies. They love them, nurse them and mold them. Finally, they push them out of the nest to grow up and start a new generation in the cycle of life. Baby eagles at some point take flight. This is when mother eagles repopulate the nest with new eaglets. The cycle of nurturing starts over again because it's built in nature. God controls all things in His own ways.

It is even more powerful when you think of mothers who exemplify love throughout the lives of their children. One of most important things she can do in saving the life of her child, is to introduce them to Jesus Christ. She urges them to salvation encouraging them to receive Jesus in their heart and baptism by water and the Spirit. I know this because my testimony is that my mother took all her children to get saved and baptized. She was successful by the Holy Spirit.

Lois and Eunice, Timothy's mother and grandmother taught him about the Lord. Then he became a preacher, recognized by the leadership of Apostle Paul. His mentor told him to be encouraged and to stir up the gift inside of him. A mother loves you, so accept Jesus right now and do it publicly. Jesus says, "Do not be ashamed of Me". His arms are open wide. You can bless someone else right after he blesses you. Watch the domino effect. Somebody saw you and now they will want to be born again. Believe in Jesus' death, burial and resurrection. God loves you.

FEAR FIGHTERS

2 Timothy 1:7 For God hath not given us the spirit of fear; but of power, and of love, and of a sound mind.

The greatest asset of a fear fighter is Jesus. The power of overflowing love through my Lord, Jesus dominates all things. The Apostle did not want Timothy to be afraid of this ministry and the challenges that lay ahead. He knew that Pharisee-minded people, non-believers, false teachers and those opposing truth and doctrine would surface to attack. Nothing can stop the power of God's overflowing love in a person's life and the ministry of Jesus Christ. Every good thing is contained in our Lord. Another advantage of a fear fighter is he/she uses weapons of warfare. A fear fighter must have on the whole armor of God to be effective in his or her aggressiveness. He/she should never feed nor give the enemy power by letting him think you are filled with fear. They can advance against the enemy when they need to. I recently saw some footage of the heavy weight champion of the world in 1988, Mike Tyson. I remembered his early victories were due to his opponents entering the ring already filled with fear. He already had the victory because of their fear. He was knocking all of them out. Most of those defeated were filled with fear that they brought with them when they stepped into the ring. In the spiritual world, you can speak victory over all enemies because

God did not give you a spirit of fear. He gave you the spirit of power, love, and a sound mind.

Some of the most heroic acts in history were demonstrated during and immediately after the attack on the twin towers, World Trade Center in New York City on September 11, 2001. The pentagon was also hit by a plane. There were multiple heroes that went inside the twin towers to save people from fire after terrorists used aircrafts to fly directly into the buildings. The enemy had struck a blow like never seen before in the heart of America and its people. The power of love rose up inside of the heroes. On that day, those heroes moved into action, immediately and saved lives. Fear did not affect firefighters and many others who went into action. Some were never mentioned as heroes. However, a hero is someone who carries people to safety, cares for them and does something that express love from the heart. Heroes aren't easily forgotten. The terrorists did not win. Love won and it still wins today. Fire fighters became an entirely different level of human hero after Sept 11, 2001. Many of them were called upon to fight the California fires, over so many years. All the firefighters and people helping to respond are heroes. I just saw a special last night on television of a firefighter who spoke of what his group thought would be the last day of their lives, as they went to fight the blazes of the California wildfires. He was injured badly. His new lease on life is that he has received Jesus Christ as Lord and

He knows that there is a God who loves Him. He was able to live another day to see his wife and baby boy. One glimpse of something like that can change something on the inside of you. Firefighters overcome fear and save people they don't even know instinctively, it is love and courage of the firefighters that motivate them. It is love and courage that caused lives to be saved. One man took a lady from the top floor to the bottom. He never knew her name. Many other cases were similar. There were so many people helping to save other people in various ways. I call all these heroes, "Fear Fighters." They earned the name fear fighters in my book and I plan on asking that a movie be made called Fear Fighters in the name of Jesus Christ. In fact, I dedicate this book and the next book to my Lord Jesus Christ and all His heroes, in Jesus name, Amen.

In 2 Timothy 1:7 it points out that God gave us power, love, and a sound mind. What does the scripture really mean? When someone gives you something, you are supposed to use it. God gave those three characteristics to every believer, so that each Christian would remain equipped through challenges. God also gave gifts and talents to us, that must be used (I Corinthians 12:4-11, 14:12-40). Becoming a fireman and using those talents and skills is crucial to others, because you are called to rescue people in dangerous situations.

As Christians, we are not to walk in fear. We are to walk with power, love and a sound mind to dominate over fear and every stronghold of the enemy. We are empowered in all three areas to live the Christian life. God has a plan for each person. The power indicates that we have faith in God working in us and through us. These three areas given to us are intended to elevate us over fear. We do not acknowledge having a spirit of fear. It has no place in our lives. If you are not careful, the enemy will exploit you by allowing the power of fear to control you. Do not accept anything from the enemy! The enemy will try to cripple your life permanently, if you allow it. Rebuke the enemy in Jesus name! Jesus wants us to have power, love and a sound mind to overcome all attacks and circumstances against our lives. He wants us to have power against all enemies and principalities (Ephesians 6:10-17). You live the Christian life now. Angels guard your life. Acknowledge Jesus as your Lord and Savior. Angels guarded my life even when I rode a 750 Kawasaki motorcycle and numerous cars almost hit me.

We, as Christians, must acknowledge and walk in the power of the Holy Spirit, the spirit of love, and take on the mind of Christ. This is a disciplined and spiritual mindset. When you take on the mind of Christ, nothing can stop you. When you walk in the spirit of love which is in Jesus Christ, no weapon formed against can break you. It is time to ask Jesus to take root of your mind. Make your requests known to Jesus to manifest His power through your mind. It's time to walk in boldness like the Apostle Paul. It's time to ask Jesus to help you walk in love. When you grasp the fact that Jesus poured out His love for you, you will be an overcomer and a warrior in His name.

As I watched the Ultimate Fighting Championship (UFC) last night, a fighter came on with a logo on his T-shirt referencing these words, fear fighters. It was not exactly that phrase but I took away from it the words "fear fighters" which mean to be ready to get in the ring and fight, whatever that fight might be. I saw it as one of those spiritual moments. The fighter defeated the previous champion by just chipping away and staying consistent with his punches at the opponent. It looked like he was going to have difficulty, but he managed to get the victory over the previous champ. He stood on his motto "fear fighter" and never wavered for a moment in the ring.

I noticed a scene in a movie entitled, "The Green Lantern." The leader was testing the new strength of the Green Lantern. He was training him and at the same time teaching him to get over fear. At one point, the leader of the empire said to him, "I smell fear in you!" It was designed to let him know that his weakest point as a hero was fear. He needed to overcome it or the enemy would take him out. In fact, the leader spoke and said he was not worthy to wear the green lantern ring.

Jesus is looking for some fear fighters in His corner. I wonder what God is saying about those who give up in God's service to win souls into the kingdom. Do not ever give up on God. Will you win some souls today for the Kingdom of God? Or are you filled with fear? Break out of it now in the name of Jesus Christ and be set free! You can do it! I promise you can do it in the name of Jesus. Come fear fighter and put the devil under your feet! Keep praying daily that the Lord continues to strengthen you. As you walk in faith you will receive the blessings. Remember the three things that will help you to become a fear fighter: 1. Accept Jesus as Lord and Savior, 2. Have a repentant heart, 3. Be obedient to God in all things.

Questions and Answers:

1. List 3 things that will help you to become a fear fighter.

_____

_____

_____

2. What do you see happening to Timothy in the scriptures?

_____

_____

3. What is a fear fighter to you?

_____

_____

Love Over Temptation

Matthew 4:1-4 Then Jesus was led by the Spirit into the wilderness to be tempted by the devil. After fasting forty days and forty nights, he was hungry. The tempter came to him and said, "If you are the Son of God, tell these stones to become bread." Jesus answered, "It is written: 'Man shall not live on bread alone, but on every word that comes from the mouth of God."

Your love for Jesus is an important factor that will help you overcome temptation. Stop and think everything through before you plan. Every decisive moment in life counts regardless of what it is. The devil did not hesitate to try to put temptation before Jesus, the son of the living God. Jesus is God in the flesh. God can't sin, Jesus can't sin, and the Holy Spirit can't sin. So, since He's perfect and can't sin, His spirit is not tempted, nor does He fall into temptation.

Jesus was on a forty day fast in the wilderness. Jesus was obeying His father and was still walking in love for His Father. Then the devil came to Jesus to try his best to tempt Him and make Him give in to temptation. Temptation did not work on Jesus. Read the scripture passage above. There are several moments of temptation in the Bible. Temptation is the desire of something or to do something wrong or unwise according to Webster's dictionary. Temptation is associated with seduction, the act of giving in to sin, luring someone into doing wrong for evil's gain. A simple example is Adam and Eve in the Garden. They were seduced by Satan to eat from the tree of the knowledge of good and evil (Genesis 2:16-17). They succumbed. Jesus did not desire anything the devil presented before Him. If I have the slightest desire for sex with a woman in my heart, I am tempted. However, when I act on it, I fall into that temptation. Falling into sin is a sign of defeat. The devil wins when we give into temptation. If we put our hearts and minds on Jesus, we have the power to walk in obedience. The scriptures remind us to submit to God, resist the devil and he will flee from us (James 4:7). Then we have the victory.

King David was one of God's anointed kings in the Bible. In fact, He was known as a man after God's own heart. Moreover, King David is also one the most recognized men in the Bible known to have given in to temptation. It appears in society that sex is the number one thing that causes people to fall into temptation. Money is also a big tempter. King David saw Bathsheba and his heart and flesh spiraled out of control with lustful desire.

Temptation was so powerful that he decided to kill her husband, Uriah the Hittite, a man at war for King David's Army. King David gave General Joab a letter from Uriah to send him to the front line in the heat of battle, so he would be killed. This was to cover up his sin with Uriah's wife, Bathsheba. He committed an act of evil to the deepest of the heart. King David fasted after the devil had cause him to have sex with another man's wife and commit murder. There are different views as to Bathsheba's innocence in this story. The bottom line is that she gave in to King David knowing that she was married. It is said that she was on a balcony type high building as required for her bath. Some think she was in a spirit of seduction to lure him in. The same attack happened in the story of Joseph, Jacob's son. It happened while Joseph was under Potiphar's command and in his house. Potiphar's wife was forcing herself sexually onto Joseph. Thankfully, Joseph was smart enough to resist her urgings. Joseph ended up running for his dear life. Joseph wanted to stay honorable to God. He wanted to remain respectful to Potiphar as well. We should all keep our eyes and hearts completely on Jesus. 1 John 2:16 tells us that "For everything in the world- the lust of the flesh, the lust of the eyes, and the pride of life-comes not from the Father but from the world." Let God be everything you need. You can do it! Joseph's integrity paid off later. Joseph received his own beautiful wife and children.

Bobby and Bridget dated for 3 years. Bridget looked like a super model, she caught his eye immediately. Bobby fell head first in love with Bridget. Bridget felt the same way about him. This was the girl of his dreams! Every time they saw one another they were tempted to express themselves, sexually. Bridget wanted to wait until after high school when a diamond ring was placed on her finger.

They attended prom night together. Bobby had one drink with his boys outside, behind the building. Bridget's girl friend told her that if she did not have sex with Bobby soon, somebody else would. Debra Miller said," It might be me since I've always had a crush on Bobby." When it was time to take Bridget home, she and Bobby got inside the car and had sexual relations on that prom night. A few weeks later, Bridget discovered she was pregnant. Both of them were about to be parents at the age of 18. Sometimes, temptation can overwhelm a person and cause them to give in without realizing the true consequences. It does not mean that every poor choice made causes them to be a bad person. It does mean when you gave in to temptation, in most cases, you will have to live with the consequences, especially if it's a baby. It also means you have a responsibility. The best thing to do is to seek God for direction in life. God still blesses you regardless of how hard things seem. God blesses babies. That is one reason we dedicate them to the Lord.

Ronnie and Laura met the other night at the dance. Ronnie thought he was in love. Ronnie has already strategized what he was going to do with Laura. At that dance, Ronnie decided to take one drink and get a buzz. He had already attended an alcohol anonymous group for a car accident. Without Laura realizing the condition and danger she was in, she got into Ronnie's car. They immediately drove off. Ronnie looked at his cell phone while he was driving intoxicated and an 18-wheeler almost hit them head on. Ronnie swerved enough to make the car flip at least 7 times before hitting a huge oak tree. Laura was thrown out of the car. Ronnie had broken his back and legs. He was paralyzed from the neck down. He also had a permanent brain injury leaving him in a coma. Laura was scarred. She had a broken arm and ribs, along with a head injury that left her in a coma. It was 8 months later when she came out of that coma and realized where she was for the last several months. After speaking with her mom, and some other women at the hospital, who were praying for her, she accepted Jesus into her life.

BE A TESTIMONY!

Revelation 12:11 And they overcame him by the blood of the Lamb, and by the word of their testimony; and they loved not their lives unto the death.

There is testimony after temptation and trials. What is your testimony? We tell everyone about Jesus Christ as our Lord and Savior, the one who redeemed us with the power of His blood. I am born again and a believer because of Him. He died for me and the world.

Psalm 71:15-18 My mouth shall shew forth thy righteousness and thy salvation all the day; for I know not the numbers thereof. I will go in the strength of the Lord GOD: I will make mention of thy righteousness, even of thine only. O God, thou hast taught me from my youth: and hitherto have I declared thy wondrous works. Now also when I am old and greyheaded, O God, forsake me not; until I have shewed thy strength unto this generation, and thy power to everyone that is to come.

Psalm 66:16 Come and hear, all ye that fear God, and I will declare what he hath done for my soul.

Matthew 10:32 Whosoever therefore shall confess me before men, him will I confess also before my Father which is in heaven.

1 Peter 3:15-16 But sanctify the Lord God in your hearts: and be ready always to give an answer to every man that asketh you a reason of the hope that is in you with meekness and fear: Having a good conscience; that, whereas they speak evil of you, as of evildoers, they may be ashamed that falsely accuse your good conversation in Christ.

1 John 1:1-4 That which was from the beginning, which we have heard, which we have seen with our eyes, which we have looked upon, and our hands have handled, of the Word of life; (For the life was manifested, and we have seen it, and bear witness, and shew unto you that eternal life, which was with the Father, and was manifested unto us;) That which we have seen and heard declare we unto you, that ye also may have fellowship with us: and truly our fellowship is with the Father, and with his Son Jesus Christ. And these things write we unto you, that your joy may be full.

Matthew 5:16 Let your light so shine before men, that they may see your good works, and glorify your Father which is in heaven.

THE GIFT OF GOD

John 4:9-10 Then the woman of Samaria said to Him, "How is it that You, being a Jew, ask a drink from me, a Samaritan woman?" For Jews have no dealing with Samaritans. Jesus answered and said to her, "If you knew the gift of God, and who it is who says to you, Give Me a drink, you would have asked Him, and He would have given you living water.

This scripture reveals a woman in need of the Savior in her life. It's a chance and moment to fall in love with Jesus. Falling in love is good for all men and women, especially if Jesus Christ is the one you fall in love with. It's powerful because He is the greatest gift that God gave. In Jesus, love will overflow in unimaginable ways. In fact, overflowing love defined in these passages means non-stop flowing of love, over the top flowing as in spilling over from a vase or container. In this case, the love of Jesus Christ is overflowing in your heart, spirit, your soul, mind. God's overflow of love has no limits. Jesus tells us in Matthew 22:36-38 to love Him with all your heart, mind, soul, strength.

The overflow of love is a constant gift from God. His love transcends time and all of creation. His love is placed inside of us by His power and design of mankind. There is no seal or regulator on the power of love. Love is in constant overflow. Love is so powerful. God has the right match for you. We must avoid all temptation and lust. Lust can disguise itself as love. Lust overflowing can mislead a person and cause devastation with the wrong choice of a husband or wife. Be careful of being alone with women or men that try to seduce you. Seduction is Satan's scheme and strategy. He uses it to bring down marriages. Lust has a certain evil power. I believe lust is attractive and can send the wrong message. Look away before the heat is turned on and turned up. It is easy for the spirit of seduction to make you yield to it. If you think seduction does not have power, then you are blind and will walk right into a trap. Even the one with the power of seduction may not realize it.

You need to remember that the love of Jesus overflows. It is in your life to help and protect. Get in and stay in the right position, so you can overcome all challenges. Avoid all traps from the demon of lust. A pretty face and a knock out, super model body can easily lure you into a sexual relationship that you did not expect. Please be advised damage will occur if you give in. Joseph shows us exactly what to do when being offered sex from a woman that is not your wife. Joseph, the son of Jacob showed every man the proper technique. This technique to get away from seduction is called run as fast as you can. He ran as fast as he could. He was still accused by Potiphar's wife and had to pay by going to prison. Nevertheless, the truth prevailed.

We need to ask God for directions. Ask God for a blessed wife. Ask God for a blessed husband. You are asking God for someone to love that has God's favor on their life. You want them to know God and have a personal relationship with Him. Make sure she/he is the right one. Falling in lust is not healthy. It can be hurtful, troubling, and painful, leaving deep scars. Avoid that kind of relationship. Just turn it off now. Look away and put your mind on Jesus. You need someone you can fall in love with. You do not want a complainer, or someone who does not honor you. Love shows respect and reverence.

The woman at the well may have thought she was in love, when she was in those past relationships. She seems to struggle between the spirit of love, lust, and loneliness. Sometimes people can be in love, but it may be with the wrong person. These three areas can confuse a person who is simply in need of real love. Loneliness can force your hand to get the wrong brother. Jesus knew He would meet this woman at the well. He knew even more about her than she thought He knew. It blew her mind when Jesus told this woman that she had five previous relationships with men, and the one she is currently with, she is not even married to. She may have already had a complex issue with knowing how Jews view Samaritans and women, to say the least.

In one respect, Jesus was informing her of her previous lifestyle and her current lifestyle. He wanted her to get her life together. In another respect, Jesus wanted her to know that He is the Son of God and that He could impact her life. He could provide her with the right husband, not just any old person who wants to get over on her. He also let her know that she is forgiven and that if only she believes in the One she is speaking to as the Son of God, her whole life could turn around. Jesus wanted her to accept Him, not those other men who meant her no good. Have you ever been there before? God helped you out of a situation to set you free. Don't go back to foolishness. Unclean spirits want to take you down by blinding you and leading into a hellish relationship. God wants you to have life and have it more abundantly. The Lord Jesus wants you to have His overflowing love in your life. Speak to Jesus! Ask Him to speak to your heart!

The lady at the well was blown away and she believed what Jesus told her. She originally thought He was a prophet. She went back and told others that she met a man who told her everything about herself, without condemning. He was offering himself to her and at the same time encouraging her to break away from a sin-filled life. Jesus was offering her love! She was better than a low self-esteem mentality. She was better than the lustful life she was living.

Some people have gotten STDs over a lust filled moment. Again, it's important that you know lust will blind you and it's deceptive. The devil is devious. Jesus wanted this woman to know if she gave her heart to Him, she would get living water. The Spirit of the Lord and His blessings would come upon her. Likewise, His spirit will come upon her. He offers a change of life by allowing us to know that he already knows all about us. He is willing to step into our lives and make changes for us, only if we surrender to Him and love Him. Your acceptance proves a starting point for your love for Jesus. The woman at the well did not have love from those men. She was longing for it, so she reached out to anybody who would show her attention.

God gave us the ultimate gift. He gave us His Son, Jesus Christ. He is the best gift that has ever been given. He sacrificed His own Son for every person on earth to destroy the work of sin.

Much like many other people in this world who believe that someone else is better than themselves, she was in total amazement. Jesus told this Samaritan woman that, *"If you knew the gift of God, and who it is who says to you, Give Me a drink, you would have asked Him, and He would have given you living water.* Jesus could give her the power of grace, the power of forgiveness that pardons and sets people free. This living water is symbolic of rushing water that revives and restores dry land. This is showing us that grace gives support to a person who needs a spiritual life when theirs has been dried up. They need refreshing and restoring. Jesus wanted to restore her soul and spiritual life that had been broken by men. He wanted her to be comforted by His grace. All she had to do is ask Him for the living water. This living water is also symbolic of a spring of water bubbling and running continuously as in a fountain. This fountain represents the overflow of God's grace and love. His grace and love never ends. In Genesis 26:19, Isaac's servants dug in the valley and discovered a well of fresh water there.

It's time to stop searching for the wrong God and the wrong religion. If you get caught up on the wrong God, life will steer you under the devil's influence. That is exactly why Jesus is the gift to people. People that believe and recognize Jesus as Lord and Savior can have a better life. The enemy has no place in their lives. With Jesus in your life, you have a new mind that thinks positive and peaceful. You have a heart of thanksgiving. Give God the glory. If you know women that are looking for love in the wrong places, tell them that Jesus has an abundance of love waiting for them. If they give their lives to Jesus now, He can show them the love that they need. He can also provide the right man in their lives.

Questions and Discussion:

1. What issues does this woman have?
_____
_____

2. What does Jesus mean by gift?
_____
_____

3. Why is the phrase "If you knew the gift of God" so important in John 4?
_____
_____
_____

DON'T BE UNEQUALLY YOKED

2 Corinthians 6:14 Be ye not unequally yoked together with unbelievers: for what fellowship hath righteousness with unrighteousness? and what communion hath light with darkness?

Shelia had joined Scientology. Ralph had grown up attending a Baptist Church in Texas. Shelia did her best to convince Ralph that he should also convert to scientology. She believed scientology to be the best religious system. For the first 3-4 weeks, something was not settling right with Ralph as he attended. Keep in mind, she lured him in with her power of persuasion. Ralph started getting irritated at what they were teaching. It had nothing to do with the Bible. His heart did not feel right about this. He also noticed that Shelia's behavior had changed a great deal. She was no longer acting like the wife he once knew. She was acting like she was under someone's control, like she was in a cult. He told her that she needed to start going to church with him because her attitude and behavior had changed and she was being controlled by those people. She still refused because she believed that her religion was better, and she was comfortable with it. The bottom line was that she is an unbeliever in Christianity.

The marriage was at a strain until they agreed to seek counseling. They ended up speaking with a neutral marriage counselor because the marriage had reached its breaking point. To their surprise, Dr. Margret Bassett was a Christian marriage counselor. She would introduce the scripture (2 Corinthians 6:14) and share an experience of a couple she knew who survived this kind of pressure in their marriage. She explained that light and darkness have no relationship together. She had to go further in her counseling as to who is the head of the house and the importance of working as a team. She even explained that if one believes and the other is not a believer in Jesus Christ, they could remain in the marriage. The hope is that the believer will win the unbeliever over to Jesus Christ. Their relationship will improve when they are on one accord and equally yoked (1 Corinthians 11:3; 1 Peter 3:1-7).

Regardless as to who is the head of the house, the relationship still needs to be on one accord and equally yoked. She had them to engage in discussion of what bothered each person, the most. She offered prayer with both and she prayed in Jesus's name. This couple was already made aware prior to the counseling, that Dr. Bassett was a Christian counselor. She put a lot of emphasis on communication. She asked them to live like they are married to each other rather than a religion. This was a healthy counseling session. In some respects, by meeting this counselor the couple really met Jesus, because this counselor pointed them to Jesus to help turn their marriage around. The counselor wanted this couple to know that you can go from a bad situation to God's love overflowing in every part of your life.

Correct any unequally yoked situation, when you know action is needed. Ask the persons involved if they plan to have a relationship with God. Show them the way. A Christian wife can win her husband to Christ (1 Peter 3). Likewise, the husband can do the same as he takes care of her (Ephesian 5). They don't have to head towards divorce. Think on the word of God. Speak the word of God. The counselor pointed that out in this verse, an unbeliever has an outside effect that opposes Jesus Christ love for marriage. If you think sex will win him, you are in a danger zone. Stop thinking that and don't do it.

This counselor told the couple they needed to be equally yoked. The huge challenge in any relationship is godliness verses ungodliness between the two people in the marriage. It causes too much trouble, loss of trust and a possible broken or failed relationship. There is a sense of not feeling loved. Love overflowing is received when you know your deepest relationship is in Jesus Christ. When you are equally yoked or in agreement, the power of overflowing love can take over your life and relationship. Blessings will be so numerous, they will overflow in your life.

The woman at the well (and perhaps someone you know in the

same predicament) was in a precarious situation (John 4). You do not have to find yourself in the same place. When you make a decision about a sexual relationship, blood line and genes are involved. Blood conditions are involved. Blood transfer is involved. Sexually transmitted diseases could be involved. Think before you have sexual relations with anyone. This male or female can be dangerous in many ways to your life. It is a serious decision. You make the calls in your life. When you do, you can close off the opportunity for spirits coming into your life, persuading you to make unwise and foolish choices.

Infatuation can literally drive you crazy, especially when the feelings aren't mutual. Do not allow Satan to win. Let no one else make a call for you, except the Holy Spirit. You need to constantly pray and consult God. People can only try to direct and advise you. The Holy Spirit gives you sound counsel. He already sees what is good for you. He will never set you up for failure. The woman at the well and the men she was once involved with were all different with different spirits. How do I know? Read it. Those relationships did not last. They were unequally yoked. She was not equally yoked with any of those men. How do I know? The story points out that she is not in relationship with any of those men.

Light and darkness do not mix. Consider when you turn on a light switch on the wall and turn it off at night time, then turn it back on. Observe what the light does. It clears all the darkness. It does not mix! Don't fool yourself into a love affair or future relationship with someone with an unrighteous spirit just because your body is in a high degree of lust. It is important that you understand the word righteousness. Righteousness means having a right standing with God. Unrighteousness is the opposite; the person has no good standing with God. This person is a nonbeliever. Therefore, your relationship will consist of constant fighting, mistrust, and other challenges. It could possibly be dangerous. Open your eyes to the truth. The opposite is living in the blessed life. Choose it, instead of trouble.

If you are trying to win someone, it's understood that you will have a conversation, but do not compromise. You have a Godly character. The power of the Holy Spirit will help you. Otherwise, the other person could lead you into unrighteousness or into darkness. The Bible discourages us from being unequally yoked. Don't fool yourself. Seek God in all matters pertaining to life and love relationships. The scripture passage above is about idolatry as it concerns relationships with the wrong person, especially connecting with someone with a dark spirit. God has already equipped you to discern right and wrong spirits. You do not have to be so highly spiritual to have a spirit of discernment. You need to exercise it, because all kinds of challenges arise in relationships.

One common problem is the assumption that a woman will somehow change a man. He will be delivered from all his issues. In reality, he ends up putting more weight on her life. She, then, starts looking old and weighed down. She has a loss of peace and joy with bags and wrinkles under her eyes. Likewise, the man can get into an unequally yoked relationship with a woman who brings in so much baggage to the point of losing his hair, mind, spirit, sense of direction, and relationship with God. An unhealthy or wrong relationship can cause you to have a heart attack. The problem in both cases is that domestic violence occurs more often when you are unequally yoked. Unequally yoked, again, means two different spirits within a relationship. One spirit can be a witchcraft spirit, in some cases. Another spirit can be a Christian spirit. Imagine that both people in this relationship are trying to make it work. This does not apply to those caught up in homosexuality or transgender relationships. If God wanted you to be a certain gender, He would have created you that way. Unequally yoked applies to any relationship including homosexual relationships which is an abomination before God (Romans 1:18-32).

You can make a person an idol and not realize that they have a dark spirit because you are deeply in a fantasy world or lusting after them. A spirit of lust can take you in the wrong direction (Galatians 5). In Galatians 5:18, several damages can occur because it speaks of lust and orgies, the flesh and witchcraft spirits that will lure you in and take you over. You need to break every stronghold now by faith in Jesus Christ. There are consequences to lust. Quick note to you and maybe most important note: blood or semen coming from another person into your body and fluid exchange is critical because there is a transfer that remains. The most important warning is HIV or AIDS disease transfer. There are other diseases as well. HIV and other diseases come from the devil. You are to be aware of his attacks and manipulation, and deceit. You must think every situation through for your benefit. Think before you allow sexual contact to your body. I recommend a blood test and marriage before you allow someone to be with you sexually.

Wanting more sex or expecting it from the beginning can easily blind you. There is a power struggle in sex with unequally yoked relationships. Jealousy and betrayal are the top two. The enemy specializes in luring girls into exalting men that live a life of darkness and the same applies to guys being lured into a relationship with women who have a spirit of witchcraft. They are all on the dark side! The problem with this relationship is that one person has the love of God inside their heart and the other person does not. That means something else is inside the heart and guiding that person's life. It is a dark spirit. The Holy Spirit and dark spirits will never commune together. Communion is a celebration and a remembrance of our Lord Jesus Christ. Our minds are fixed on our relationship with him. It's coming together to share something in common in praise and worship. God does not share love relationships with a dark spirit (evil). It is impossible for them to be equally yoked.

Can you see it now? If you are a child of God, someone living in darkness is not equally yoked with you. Unless both of you accept Jesus as Lord and Savior, you will be unequally yoked and domestic violence will increase for the worst. Demonic spirits will enter your place and your life. If you accept Jesus, true love, peace and joy comes into the relationship. You learn to rest in Jesus.

Another huge problem is deception. The deception comes in when a woman thinks that she has arrived by having a baby with a man who seems to live a fantasy life. He may have a high price lifestyle (yacht and jet), an impressive profession, and be charismatic. But if he never speaks of God's blessing in his life, he is bad news. This person is probably an atheist, one who does not believe in God. He always has an argument against who Jesus is, like he is so intelligent, but he knows nothing. He does not have eternal life. This person could easily set you up for a big trap. Note that this person does not honor God and you are in his company, hanging out. If they have not accepted Jesus as Lord and Savior and confess it, then you need to run. Yes, you figured it out, it's a trap. You might be laughing, but do not stay there. Get out now. Ask questions and get to know something about the person to whom you are attracted. You will know if this person is satisfying in God's sight. Therefore, do not be in a big rush to commit your body and be intimate with someone you are not equally yoked with.

You should not have sex before marriage or you might end up pregnant. Sex outside of marriage is disobedience. It is called fornication. You need to know why this person is not a Christian. He needs to be one who believes in Jesus Christ as Lord and Savior, the only one who died on the cross and rose from the grave. I was watching a show one day and a woman was mesmerized by a male foreigner. She instantly took to this man from another country and had babies for him. This foreigner was evil and acted like a taskmaster toward her, treating her like a slave. She had no clue what she was getting into. Lust will make you blind! He was extremely strict and violent in his religious belief as a Muslim. She was a Christian. It was her lust that caused her to tie herself to him. The spirit of seduction does not just attack men, it attacks women also. Many women fall for men they call "cute." This lady tied herself to the wrong man. He beat her and held her hostage. You see his belief was not a belief in Jesus Christ, freedom and love. It was a bondage belief system. His behavior was erratic. He was from a foreign country and different culture, but cute in her eyes. Be careful who you think you are in love with. When you are unequally yoked, hell can break out at any time. You need to know if this person is into fortification and adultery. You need to know if this person just wants to have sex with you as a one-night stand or is this your future husband?

Questions and Discussions

1. What does it mean to be unequally yoked?
_____
_____

2. Who should be equally yoked and why?
_____

3. Who in the scripture is 2 Corinthians 6:14 referring to as unequally yoked?
_____
_____

GOD RESTORES MARRIAGE

God can build and restore your marriage. Let's be crystal clear first and foremost. You are responsible for receiving the restorative power of God for your individual life, before your marriage is repaired. Let's also be clear that each person needs to be obedient to God. If you want this restoration in your life and marriage, you will have to follow the leading of the Holy Spirit. Examine yourself. You might be the problem. As in all cases, one of you or both of you may be the problem. The solution is obedience to the Holy Spirit.. Start reading the Word of God. Start obeying what it says. For example, Ephesians 5:24-25 says "For the husband is the head of the wife, even as Christ is the head of the church: and he is the Savior of the body. Therefore as the church is subject unto Christ, so let the wives be to their own husbands in everything." Follow the word of God! It is time for you to admit where you fall short and ask God to build you, shape and mold your life. He is the potter. Ask Him to help you to obey and to submit to one another in marriage (Ephesians 5:23-28).

I watched a movie called, "Fireproof" in which the main character used a book called "Love Dare". It helped the marriage get restored using the power of love and Godly patience. The marriage was headed to destruction until the husband took responsibility to make it work. He ended up making his wife feel like a real woman of God and His queen. He was working on building the covenant in his marriage. Ask God to make your marriage strong and holy. When you join together in marriage, it is permanent (Genesis 2:24-25). Both the husband and wife need Jesus. You need to be born again (John 3:3). You need to know love in your heart. There are several areas that need to be addressed. But three key issues that should be observed in marriages are: pornography, the lack of trust and the absence of intimacy.

I'm writing this because there are so many solutions to repair and restore marriage. One solution is to submit to each other respectfully in love. This can cease all issues of pornography and adultery immediately. Your relationship is in God's design (Genesis 2, 3). You must ask God in prayer to guide your relationship. It is important to have respect and honor for each other, then the relationship will be strong and honorable. Everything will fall in place because God is in it. The man has an obligation to ease the mind of his wife by no longer watching pornography. I'm going to give 4 solutions for you to restore your marriage, if you want it restored. God can equip you to take back your marriage in Jesus name!

Solution #1. Keep your husband/wife occupied with intimacy in the bedroom and time spent alone together! Remember, it is about both of you! No one else should be involved in your marriage intimacy and time alone. Don't allow anyone else to tamper with your love for your spouse. How do you do it? Spend quality time with your mate rather than other people.

Make your quality time count! Set scheduled times and at other times be spontaneous and gentle with one another. A husband should be spontaneous and surprise his wife with flowers or jewelry. Tell your spouse that you love them often. If a husband is not as spontaneous as you want him to be, do not get upset with him. Do not make him feel like he messed up, so bad. Avoid feeling disappointment. Some disappointment can mean that it's all about you. The thing is he may already be trying to make it about you. Some women know it, and some miss it! Find out what is needed with each other to be happy. Value the love in your relationship between you and your husband. If you're concerned about your sexual intimacy level and relationship, do something about it. Get involved with your husband, sexually, several days out of the week until both of you are secure, confident and satisfied. Some of the issues in marriage stem from lack of security and falling short in intimacy. One lady was speaking on the radio that she was doing all the right things in her relationship and it still had issues. That is a red flag! It's a red flag because talk is cheap on the radio and among friends or talking to a therapist. Taking genuine action is the key. So, act today!

Solution #2 Spend the whole day together. If you must, take time off from work and your friends. Take time off from whatever things you may have put before your wife. Wives, likewise, spend time with your husband. This will increase intimacy in your marriage.

Solution #3 Stop complaining about things between each other. Stop blaming each other and fix it. Tell each other what you like. Be positive about your spouse. Be very sensitive and loving when you share issues. Good communication is one of the highest keys to a relationship. Communicate a solution to each other, as to what will make you happy. Keep in mind that God is the center of your marriage and your intimacy. God invented sexuality and intimacy. He designed man and woman with organs for pleasure and reproduction. It is good in God's sight. Nothing should be broken. If your relationship is not restored after these solutions, there is a good chance you didn't want your relationship to work. If it is restored, it's because you wanted a happy and healthy blessed marriage and you were willing to put in the work. A reality check is needed. Do you really want it, or are you going through the motions? If so, stop placing a blame if something is broken on your end. If you love each other communicate and make love happen. Go to your private place and make love. Jesus is your solution to all your intimacy issues. God created sex to be a beautiful thing between a husband and wife. It is design to love and produce!

Solution #4. Kiss and hug at least at least 2 to 3 times a day. Give each other real kisses and hugs more than twice a day. Do it in the morning. If you can for lunch, that's great. Hug and kiss when it's time to go to bed, at night. Your relationship is valuable. Men and women need to stop with all the excuses. Do not manipulate him or her. Rebuke any and all things that get in the way. There should be zero excuses. Wives, don't worry about your husbands. They have nothing to hide behind. Hopefully, once he sees you, his mind is already blown. Remember men are more visual, women are more emotional. And they both have serious emotional and social needs.

Solution #5 play together and love on each other. Have fun together. It is vital that you drop anyone who tries to hinder your relationship. Women if you're looking at another man, turn your eyes away. Men if you are looking at a provocative and seductive woman, turn your head. Repent and ask the Lord to help you overcome lust. The only thing that can save that marriage is a made-up mind after you consult Jesus. Pray and ask God to heal that marriage. No marriage is restored unless Jesus is in every one of these steps. If you want a broken marriage restored, Jesus must be the center of your life men.

LOVE OVERFLOW MANIFESTED

1 John 4:8 Whoever does not love, does not know God, because God is love

Overflowing love was already inside God. The Bible is very simple at pointing this out. According to 1 John 4:8, God is love. Everything about God is from a foundation of love. In fact, because He is God, love exists to manifest power in the life of creation that God made. Therefore, the overflow had to begin when God started releasing His love on humanity and all that He created (Genesis 1, 2, 3). He has unlimited love and impact on the life of man and creation (Genesis 2:7). Adam had so much love inside of him that God had to put him to sleep and give him a woman (helper) so he could receive love in an intimate way (Genesis 2:22). This is written because most wives don't understand their true purpose for their husband. It was a blessing and gift for Adam to receive her (Genesis 2:22-24).

Intimacy is not just about sex! It is about a deeper relationship involving love, sex, communication and trust. Some of the most powerful examples of God's love overflowing is the virgin birth of Jesus Christ, Jesus dying on the cross for man's redemption and salvation, and the resurrection of the risen Lord, Jesus Christ. God reveals to all mankind His overflowing love through powerful evidence of His love manifested, Jesus Christ, the Son of God.

ONE ACCORD

Matthew 18: 5-6 And said, for this cause shall a man leave father and mother, and shall cleave to his wife: and they twain shall be one flesh? Wherefore they are no more twain, but one flesh. What therefore God hath joined together, let not man put asunder.

The true power of being one flesh in a marriage defeats all enemy attacks. Being one puts you in a spiritual one accord relationship. Nevertheless, Jesus Christ must be the center. This kind of relationship brings about a being on one accord simply means walking in sync, living a synchronized relationship in a spirit of agreement. It represents a true covenant marriage. You signed a marriage certificate in agreement. You promised your life to each other before God.

You communicate in your marriage. You pray to God and hear His voice and obey it. One accord reinforces a couple's love relationship. The most powerful bonding source in the marriage is Jesus Christ. If you do not have Him, make it a priority. This is the most powerful decision a couple can make. When you are one in your marriage as Genesis 2:24 and Mark 10:8 says, you are highly blessed. However, if you are married and all the time out of agreement, you are not on one accord and the enemy is seeking to destroy your relationship, as fast as he can. Your answer is to go to Jesus Christ in prayer and both of you repent and accept Jesus Christ as Lord and Savior individually. Then you become part of His Church to worship, serve and fellowship with Him. You must stop inappropriate fellowship with things outside of your marriage. Don't stop living, just adjust your lifestyle so that it is pleasing to Jesus, our Lord. You need to pray and communicate with one another. Set a time to pray together. Nothing else is more important because this involves your relationship with Jesus, as well. Usually a married couple is not on one accord because they may not have a true relationship with Jesus. Sometimes, it may be because the enemy has entered the relationship, and no one has prayed the enemy out of the relationship. You must take a stand if you want your marriage to survive. You may have stated you believe and love Jesus at the wedding ceremony, but be far from having a relationship with Him. Living on one accord is coming into agreement with Jesus. The old person that was out of agreement no longer exists with those old destructive behaviors. Why do people try so hard to be on one accord with other people outside of your marriage? It's usually because of an impression or not wanting someone to think badly of them. Please understand that your marriage is priority before anyone else. Spend the energy working on your relationship.

The most challenging piece about being on one accord is in the relationship itself, how you feel about your mate. In Mark 10 reminds us that married couples are one. *Jesus says in Mark 10:6-8 "But from the beginning of the creation God made them male and female. For this cause shall a man leave his father and mother and cleave to his wife; And they twain shall be one flesh: so, then they are no more twain, but one flesh."*

Your love for one another is stronger than any glue compound. Being on one accord is a spiritual glue that keeps couples together. You can be blessed for a lifetime. Togetherness is powerful for the family and in the eyes of God.

Real Love

When true love sets in, reality will hit you like a ton of bricks. Why? It is because love is real! When you face the fact of real love, you will stop taking things for granted in your marriage. Love is not pretentious. It is something so real to the heart that your heart will not miscalculate it! No matter how you try to shake things, love will not be shaken off! You do not have to go on live television to prove a point regarding your love for some. Nevertheless, make no mistake, you will wake up to reality when you are in love and the feelings are so strong in your heart! You will discover the power of love working in your heart toward another person that constantly stays on your mind. It takes the right woman or the right man in your life to touch your heart. Love is powerful! Ask someone who has been married for a long time. Here is something to think about. The longer you are married, the more demons try to destroy your love relationship. The attack could easily get greater when the marriage has survived for 20, 30 and over 40 years. Don't misunderstand, the attack comes against love at any stage of marriage. Just like love is real. The enemy comes. However, stop allowing the enemy to make you see your mate in a negative light. See Him or her in God's light, speak something positive, and build him up! Build her up! Let love be the center of your marriage. Love is real in Jesus Christ, the Son of God, Lord and Savior of the world.

The most important piece regarding love is when God touches your heart. Love is also mentioned in 1 Corinthians 13:13 "And now abideth faith, hope, charity (love), these three; but the greatest of these is charity (love). Then the relevance of God's love will set in immediately and over-power other things. You will fall in love with Jesus! One thing for sure God will enforce in your heart that you are born again (John 3:3). There is no condemnation to those who are in Jesus Christ (Roman 8:1-2). There is nothing like true love touching the heart. When love opens your mind, it helps you to view reality in a different light. The reality and the relevance of God is that we are bought with a price. You are not your own. God owns you. He purchased you and I on Calvary with His blood (1 Corinthian 6:18-20). As a married couple, several things become clearer in your relationship, as husband and wife. This is all relevant to your marriage and life together. It's also more relevant for your relationship in Jesus Christ.

The way you treat each other sets the present and future stages of your marriage for success or failure. It is your choice to decide. No one wants a failed marriage. The way you demonstrate and express love to one another is important. The relationship is about action between both of you especially in intimacy. The time you spend together has meaning. Life together becomes something precious. True love will make every moment a special moment together. The Lord gives you a picture of how you can bless each other in your marriage, He says "Therefore as the church is subject unto Christ, so let the wives be to their own husbands in everything. Husbands, love your wives, even as Christ also loved the church, and gave himself for it; That he might sanctify and cleanse it with the washing of water by the word, That he might present it to himself a glorious church, not having spot, or wrinkle, or any such thing; but that it should be holy and without blemish (Ephesians 5:24-27)."

This passage may help you. *1 Peter 3:1-6 Likewise, ye wives, be in subjection to your own husbands; that, if any obey not the word, they also may without the word be won by the conversation of the wives; While they behold your chaste conversation coupled with fear. Whose adorning let it not be that outward adorning of plaiting the hair, and of wearing of gold, or of putting on of apparel; But let it be the hidden man of the heart, in that which is not corruptible, even the ornament of a meek and quiet spirit, which is in the sight of God of great price. For after this manner in the old time the holy women also, who trusted in God, adorned themselves, being in subjection unto their own husbands: Even as Sara obeyed Abraham, calling him lord: whose daughters ye are as long as ye do well, and are not afraid with any amazement.*

For most people, it is at a time of loss, death in the family or a divorce when reality sets in more than ever. God is merciful and loves all people. Those moments are when the power of love means more to us than anything. The purpose of this book is to acknowledge that we need His love in every moment of life. It is for you to grab a hold of the power of God's love and not let go. We are talking about moments when you realize that the person you loved all those years had the nerve to get up and leave you for another women or man after you poured out yourself to him or her. When God intended for you to marry, it was for a lifetime. God intended for you to remain faithful. Reality sets in when you are broken and need strength. The only place you can be comforted is in the arms of God. Call on the name of Jesus for all things. Open your heart to Him and let Him inside. Stop allowing reality shows to dictate your life. Stop allowing scientology and other religions such as Buddhism, Islam and other things run your life. You need to get out of it now!! You need to ask Jesus Christ to come into your heart today. Ask God to guide your life. Salvation is free. Jesus already paid the cost for you and me!

GOD'S POWER OVER STRONGHOLDS

2 Corinthians 10:4-5 The weapons we fight with are not the weapons of the world. On the contrary, they have divine power to demolish strongholds. We demolish arguments and every pretension that sets itself up against the knowledge of God, and we take captive every thought to make it obedient to Christ.

The Apostle Paul had true and genuine boldness to minister for our Lord, Jesus. It was Jesus Christ Himself who positioned the Apostle Paul so that He could do the work pleasing in God's sight. I love the fact that the Apostle really reminds us that Jesus has the power over every stronghold. Paul's old nature's primary stronghold was that he took pleasure in killing Christians, when he was Saul. You need to understand that the old man was crucified in Jesus Christ. However, be aware that the old man tried to resurface. Jesus broke Saul out of that stronghold for His purpose while on the road to Damascus in which he discovered Jesus

Christ. Once Saul experience Jesus Christ on that road to Damascus, his life changed and become the Apostle Paul, one of the greatest Apostles ever. II Corinthians 10:4 reads, "The weapons we fight with are not the weapons of the world. On the contrary, they have divine power to demolish strongholds." Do you desire to be used by God but someone or something is holding you back? Clearly, the Lord has set us free in John 8. Therefore, nothing has power over you because whom the Son has set free is free indeed (John 8). For our struggle is not against flesh and blood, but against the rulers, against the authorities, against the powers of this dark world and against the spiritual forces of evil in the heavenly realms (Ephesians 6:12). The Bible is clear in Galatians 5:19-25 regarding a corrupt nature (Galatians 5:19-21) and a fruitful nature (Galatians 5:22-25). The Bible tells us in Colossians 3:8 to put off anger, abuse, slander, rage, and other sins that impact your life. Break free and serve Him today. This Sunday, surprise your wife or your husband. Go up and join the church when the Pastor gives an invitation. Go ahead and get activated and busy in God's Kingdom. You are blessed and highly favored.

The Holy Spirit led the Apostle Paul to be an apostle and evangelist on the missionary field by touching thousands of lives. The Holy Spirit led him to breach all lines of the enemy. His goal was to press for the prize and glorify Jesus Christ. The Apostle

Paul wanted to be pleasing in God's sight. It was Jesus who blessed the Apostle Paul to become the saint he turned out to be. I think what was important is that God placed His word in this vessel and used Him mightily.

It was the Apostle who gave us the word on Grace. In Ephesian 2:8 He reminds us that all lines are breached. The devil's camp has been breached so that saints can take back lost brothers and sisters. You can help your family break strongholds of alcohol, abuse, lying and cheating. We have a God that is so powerful and mighty who gave us grace, a gift that the enemy can't breach. Grace can't be altered. Grace can't be shattered. Grace can't be manipulated. Grace can't be stolen or lost. God owns it and allows us to preach His word, so it will not return void. Grace breaches every obstacle of the enemy and every obstacle of man's bondage and fleshly desires. God is good and worthy of all praise. That is exactly why you and I can rest in His grace. No need to worry about anything. We have grace on our side and Jesus to back it up.

In the military, it takes professionalism, training, and discipline to spot the enemy's booby traps, IEDs, and RPG launchers, that can cause massive numbers of casualties on the battle field. We have God's angels guiding and protecting us (Psalms 91). We have grace to keep us in His perfect will. We have the strong arm of the

Lord on our side. In the spiritual world, when you are in battle, it is because you either accepted Jesus as Lord of your life or you are living a lifestyle that does not please God. You can break it at any moment because of God's power and love for you. The Lord desires that you to walk as a new creature in Jesus Christ. Jesus wants you to be one of His soldiers and warriors in the kingdom. Do not allow past combat pressures to take over your life with depression, PTSD, suicide, and guilt. You are not guilty! It is not your fault in combat or at home! Our bodies experience changes due to situational stress and other factors. Never blame yourself. The enemy is the one who tries to accuse you, not God. God is helping you overcome every circumstance and accusation of the devil. Take your life back today!! You can do it! Do not allow IEDs and RPGs to stain your life, nor be a stronghold. You are in Jesus Christ now. That means you have the authority to break every strong hold, every chain, every lie, and every attack that the enemy and anyone throw at you. You belong to the King of Kings and Lord of Lords! You reign in Jesus Christ now.

Questions and Discussions

1. Which scripture in the passage will help you break strongholds?

_____

2. List strongholds that need to be broken in your life?

   _____

   _____

3. How will you better serve your family and the church after breaking strongholds?

   _____

   _____

   _____

CHAPTER 2

LOVE INTERVENTION & RESTORE

12-STEP PLAN

Matthew 19:4-6 says, "Haven't you read the Scriptures?" Jesus replied. "They record that from the beginning 'God made them male and female.'" And he said, 'This explains why a man leaves his father and mother and is joined to his wife, and the two are united into one. Since they are no longer two but one, let no one split apart what God has joined together."

Guard your marriage by ensuring Jesus is the priority. If you do not see Jesus in your marriage, you have a deep problem. One of your main priorities now is to accept Jesus Christ as your Savior. God knows already your challenges in defeating the urge to split or divorce. This is a primary reason why Jesus says, "let no one split apart what God has joined together." Everyone needs Jesus to sustain and restore their lives, broken areas in relationships and marriages. You will experience struggles, some more challenging than others. However, count on the Lord to heal and restore, no matter what. The marriage is instituted by God. The origin of family was created by God. They are one in love! Their love overflows with each person in intimacy and relationship. Put the effort into it in the name of Jesus!

There is a woman on television who usually goes door to door, using her intervention skills in helping so many families and individuals to recover and be restored from different issues of life. The intent in this book is to reveal to you that Jesus also goes door to door and is the most powerful force that exists to fix your life. Jesus operates in His own overflowing love that has all power in it.

It is important to maintain oneness in marriage to avoid a divorce or split. Every couple needs Jesus in their marriage. Some marriages are in an emergency/crisis status and must have Jesus to intervene. It will always take intervention by the Holy Spirit to straighten up your marriage. It is powerful to know that your marriage is in the oneness status according to the passage above. Oneness means that your lives are intertwined for the rest of your lives. Every problem or issue you approach must be given to the Lord to resolve. Your trust and obedience must be activated.

Nothing is more powerful than God intervening in your marriage and relationship. He is the ultimate counselor in your marriage. Your most vital step in the intervention process is to trust God and be obedient to His counsel. Trust that His love will not fail you. When love intervenes in any relationship, you can count on it being repaired in the name of Jesus Christ. You are one in this marriage. When you get off course of being one, something else causes issues., I am sure if I took a poll today on couples suffering in their marriage, they will tell you that intimacy kind of love is missing. The romance is absent! The feeling of rejection is on the rise, which is a major problem. Both are at the root cause of it because they have not allowed Jesus to come in and fix the relationship.

The same person who made you one in this marriage is the same person that can help you repair those broken areas that the enemy and your flesh caused. Sure, if you want counseling, go for it. However, keep in mind your primary counseling is God's intervention plan, which is the Holy Spirit in your life. You can have almost perfect harmony and peace in your marriage if you allow God in it! In most couple's lives, they do not have Jesus as the center of their lives. Also stop allowing anything outside of God to intrude or intervene. You may want to find a Christian counselor as well. Nevertheless, there are multiple counselors available in various communities. Choose someone with Godly wisdom.

Intervention Steps to follow:

Step 1. Pray together daily as a couple to receive Jesus Christ' intervention and restoring power.

Step 2. Lift up your husband and wife no matter what and keep it genuine.

Step 3. Seek Jesus day and night and read the word of God on love and relationships.

Step 4. Spend valuable time together no matter what, dining, events and fun days.

Step 5. Avoid and stop any negative conversation and thoughts!

Step 6. Communicate how beautiful she is and how handsome he is daily!

Step 7. Show true love with sensitivity and strong intimacy, both of you!

Step 8. Cherish every moment of love and intimacy! Let wife and husband know you are happy!

Step 9. Make love count by complimenting each other daily.

Step 10. Everything outside the marriage remains outside! It's a three-cord marriage. Jesus is the primary cord holding your marriage together. No one else impacts your marriage.

Step 11. All jobs, self-employed business should never take priority over your marriage.

Step 12. Glorify God every day of your lives individually and together.

Throughout steps 1-12, the most crucial is that you receive Jesus as Lord and Savior as the first step in this plan.

Questions:

1. What are some positive outcomes of these intervention steps? Did you involve Jesus Christ?

_____

_____

_____

2. Discuss each of these in a group setting and with husband and wife in God's presence:

A DEDICATION TO MY GENUINE FAMILY MEMBER AND PET MY ROMEO, OUR LITTLE BLESSED SON, A MINISTERING PUPPY

ROMEO FOREVER IN MY HEART

Psalm 22:24 For he has not despised or scorned the suffering of the afflicted one; he has not hidden his face from him but has listened to his cry for help.

This passage is meant to comfort in times of grieving for the loss of someone you loved. God knows exactly how to take care of any grieving heart. God knows how to handle those afflicted and experiencing suffering. Let God give comfort in every way. It is only He who know how to do it effectively with the power of love. God sees what is going on and provides that comfort and reassures us of his love and peace

Romeo, my little ministering puppy spent most of his time blessing our family with his love. We loved rubbing his silky beautiful hair! His hair was amazing. He was a handsome little man! The amazing thing is that he knew he had a purpose to minister to us.

I don't usually allow many things to affect my heart much! In fact,

I prefer, as the scripture in Proverbs 4 says to guard my heart. Nevertheless, my heart was open and Romeo got in ways I did not even imagine! The power of love is amazing and so unlimited. Ever since Romeo came into our lives, things were different in our lives and in our home. My wife and I brought home our little man and we named him Romeo, a Yorkshire terrier (Yorkie). Our new addition blessed our lives. God is so good! He was more than we ever imagined! God did it again to our hearts!

The Lord placed Romeo in our lives to help minister to our family. I really believe this little man saved my life so many times on various occasions. He was a God-sent little puppy. God is so powerful and loving to have given us Romeo. God can do that, just so you know. Romeo was filled with love, joy and such a peace that his love touched us. He was small enough to fit into my hand at birth. He also was small to fit inside of one tile square on the floor at home. From day one, my wife rubbed his little stomach and face and he would pull her hand back to him each time she tried to stop. He was spoiled from the beginning! We knew we had a smart and heart loving puppy! Romeo shared his love and joy throughout our home and wherever we took him people instantly fell in love.

Romeo was the best dog in the world to us! I still believe he helped to extend my life on earth. It's like he knew when to come up to you to remove stress, pain and whatever you were going through. This was indeed a puppy sent from God! He automatically touched people hearts. We were blessed then and still blessed in our hearts because of God giving us Romeo. Romeo was like a little son He had everybody's heart. When he was a baby, he could fit in my hand because he was so tiny. As a small puppy growing, he ran so fast on our back patio and yard that I could not catch him. I just could not believe his speed at just a few months old. Sometimes he would look up to me and just allowed me to pick him up, knowing I could catch him.

The innocence in his eyes and heart are etched inside my heart forever and make no mistake about that! God did it again. I can't get over the incredible and divine power of God in creating such creatures. Thank you, Jesus, for love in the eyes of our puppy, Romeo! Romeo meant so much to me and my wife. We will never stop thinking of Him. One thing for sure, he was a protector, companion, prayer partner, champion of love, my wife's baby, and my little man. It was so funny that he loved my wife so much that he would protect her even from my kisses. Even if I reached out to kiss her, Romeo would put up a real defense as to say back off buster! She is mine! I always found it a joy, touching, and laughed at it. Romeo was almost 9 years old. This was the most joyous, heart filling, peaceful, loving, and perfect dog, and companion I ever knew and had. This was a dog of honor. He would lick your tears and let you hold him to heal you! He was my little super man and little football star player. We had football jerseys for him and his favorite football where he loved to catch. Jesus, I love you because of what you have already done in our lives with Romeo. I must stop and thank you for Romeo and ask you to keep Him in puppy heaven as you only know how. In the beginning, when we picked up Romeo, I call myself guarding my heart from getting too close to him. It did not last a week. Romeo has already found his way into my heart as well as my wife's heart. He got in our hearts early as a baby and is still in our hearts forever! My wife wanted a puppy and she got one for both of us.

To this day, I know that God sent Romeo in our lives to save and change our lives to be better Christians. He fulfilled his purpose from God by taking a piece of my heart and saving my life at the same time! God is so awesome in His blessings! This guard dog, loving companion, little angel dog, praying dog ministered to all of us by serving his God-sent purpose. My wife called Romeo her praying puppy because he was there during her prayer times in our home. At times, Romeo would watch me pray inside my office at the altar. God has a way of sending blessings in our lives. Romeo was a dog filled with love which only God can do. Romeo was the perfect puppy, absolutely filled with joy and love from God always. In fact, to rub on his hair and top of his little head to removed stress and any problem that I seem to face on any day.

It's so powerful how God can put a pet in your life to save your life. I got so close to him that we even rubbed noses, pet his head and rubbed his back. He knew how I felt about him. Romeo brought total joy, peace, love, laughter, excitement and more into our lives. I started writing this because the thought of God's power of love for a family member and pet like Romeo hit my heart and mind with amazement. He was my little man who gave unconditional love from God to us.

When I think of Romeo giving so much love to us, it's clear to me even more as to what love means and God's power of directing it. It's when God allows His love to be felt in our hearts and seen through our own little puppy,. I call him my puppy even though he was over 9 years old. Others also experience Romeo's love when they came around him. It is the power of God's love working within us! We know only God can give unconditional love. So, his love was from our Lord, God. We did not owe him anything to be loved by him. He just knew we loved him back! This is how you know the Lord sent him in our lives, because Jesus gives us unconditional love. He would just love you through troubles and pain and anytime you needed love. For all those years His mom, my wife used to always tell him go and see your dad. She was referring to me, and I had given in and accepted that I was his daddy. It ripped my heart that Romeo had to leave on 9 Sept 2017. Truthfully, I don't think I can handle anything like this again.

It hurt too much! I prayed a blessing over him and asked Jesus to keep Romeo in His hand. Receive him in heaven Lord, God's kingdom for puppies. My wife also prayed over her little baby boy Romeo. She cried, and I cried on 9 Sept 2017 when he left us.

Today, 10 Sept 2017 on Sunday, I preached a sermon entitled "Count it all Joy." The scripture was James 1:2-4. I was thinking of the joy our puppy gave us at home. I do know that spiritual joy comes from God. God can do whatever He desires to do in your life. In this scripture, we mature through testing and trials, so God can use us. It's powerful when you know you can have joy in the Lord! Joy is most powerful coming from God. It's so powerful that God gave us Romeo to have joy and love in our lives. It powerful when you can persevere in times of pain. Romeo lives in our hearts forever. We are reminded that God brings joy so many ways. He used Romeo in our life. God wants all His Saints to know that we find joy in God's presence. In *Psalms 16:11, "You make known to me the path of life; in your presence there is the fullness of joy; at your right hand are pleasures forevermore.* We can rejoice believing that our little Romeo is running around free, no pain in perfect harmony and peace in doggy heaven where now he sees Jesus and angels in heavens doggy playground. *Ecclesiastes 3:19-21 For people and animals share the same fate, both breathe, and both must die. So, people have no real advantage over the animals. How meaningless! Both go to the same place; they came from dust and they return to dust. For who can prove that the human spirit goes up and the spirit of animals goes down into the earth?* The Bible also tells us in Psalm 50:10 for every animal of the forest is mine, and the cattle on a thousand hills. Jesus wants us to recognize who we belong to as well as animals belong to Him. What a comfort that God knows all things.

There is a lot symbolism in scripture about animals as well. *In Isaiah 11:6-9 "The wolf will live with the lamb, the leopard will lie down with the goat, the calf and the lion and the yearling together; and a little child will lead them."* God reveals in His word evidence in Ecclesiastes 3:19-21 that animals appear symbolically and exist in God's kingdom. Revelation 19:11-14 shows another picture of animals existing in the kingdom of heaven. We may see them as symbols with specific meaning to God and how God presents them. God's blessings are on all His creation for His purpose. No one can ever say that God can't do what is pleasing to Him. There is power in His love for His created animals and pets. Your pet is seen by God and has love from God inside of its heart. Only God knows everything! He knows that you are blessed, filled with joy and He knows when you need comforted. God is comforting you and me right now. Believe it! In the name of Jesus Christ.

God created every animal for His purpose. You see animals in heaven in the scripture above. God made me think of how gentle a lamb is and how people rub on lambs, adore their gentleness and innocent nature. Pets are of that gentle and innocent nature that draws the heart of people to them. Everything good orchestrated by God in the pet's heart and the human person's heart. The only way it happens is through the power of God's love for animals, pets, and people. God created pets for our hearts to love and well- being. I was reading a few months ago as I was writing this that a woman died over a broken heart because her Yorkie had passed away. At that moment, it confirmed everything about love in the heart of a human for a pet. It made me think also about the love in the pet's heart for a human. They are so intelligent and loving! God is always looking out for His people and His pets. He used an animal to serve Jesus as well. Jesus also wants us to love Him back even though He knows many have difficult believing. One single pet will help you believe in Jesus and help your move to new levels of love.

I thought I was finished writing this book until I just received a letter from a Pet Hospital in Killeen Texas in which Romeo routinely visited ever since he was first born. The letter touched my heart! This hospital gave a generous donation to the College of Veterinary Medicine & Biomedical Science at a Texas University to finance the cost of many student's professional education and minimizing animals suffering and to in various situations like disaster-stricken places and other diseases. This love attitude has opened my eyes to see that I as well as others need to get involved and support efforts in this Texas College Research and Animal Humane Society. All animals and creation belong to God.

We need the Holy Spirit to lead us to love Jesus back and serve Him. Our service in Jesus will prove our love for Him. He has a purpose for everyone to love and even gives us pets and companions to bring out the best in us and our lives. God is so powerful and loving in me and my family that I can't help but to exalt His name for all things. We thank God for blessings our little Romeo and keeping him in his hand and in puppy heaven. In Jesus name.

John 14:27 "I am leaving you with a gift, peace of mind and heart. And the peace I give is a gift the world cannot give. So, don't be troubled or afraid.

LOVE FORGIVES ALL SIN

Matthew 6:15 But if you do not forgive others their sins, your Father will not forgive your sins.

Love has the power to forgive a person of all sin. In short, the scripture is simple in form and meaning. It simply means to forgive because forgiving goes both ways. The power of forgiveness through Jesus Christ is not looking for your past sin nor your present sin. Jesus already forgave you of sin. Sin was defeated on the cross at Calvary by the death of my Lord and Savior Jesus Christ, the anointed one and Son of the living God. Why would He look for your faults and sin when He already defeated it?

The power of love matters the most. The power of love has he forgiveness within to restore a person. Love has power to bring a person back to God. Love has power to get you through any obstacle in your life. Love has sheer power to release you from any man made and evil spirit. Love has the power to set you up with the right companion. Yes, it's correct. God will provide you with a man or woman you can love. Love and forgiveness have the power to move your children into becoming Christ-like children. These kinds of children know how to identify right and wrong and avoid evil influence

God's love has the power to change a person walking in adultery and homosexuality. When you walk in homosexuality, you have an identity crisis and are the influence of an ungodly spirit. Your life is currently under a spirit of defilement because God never created sex to be used in that way. It is to be used properly like Adam and Eve was created (Genesis 2:18-25). You will never see in the Bible God approving a man to marry a man. This is a bad example for children. You send a message to a child that your sexual relationship is acceptable to God, knowing in your heart that it is not true. It has always been from the beginning of creation - one man and one woman together to produce children (Genesis 1:27-28) (Romans 1).

It is the love of God that pull you out of all those circumstances in life. One situation in the Bible comes to mind is the story of Joseph. I recall reading that Potiphar's wife wanted to have sex with Joseph, but he denied her because he was an honorable man of God.

Joseph, the dreamer had God on his side in all circumstances even when it looked like he did not. Joseph was thrown in prison due to Potiphar's wife falsely accusing Joseph of trying to force himself on her. The circumstances looked bad, but God was on Joseph's side. Remember when it was all said and done, Joseph came out of the prison and was selected by Pharaoh to interpret dreams and he became the second highest position in all of Egypt because of Joseph's God. Joseph had the spirit of forgiveness, truth, wisdom and humbleness before the Lord to others. He even forgave his brothers for throwing him into a pit. Listen, Joseph's heart was on God constantly. Therefore, God saw fit to take Joseph from the pit and prison to the palace.

Apostle Paul wrote 13 books in the Bible and went on several missionary journeys to preach Jesus. It was the power of forgiveness from Jesus that converted Saul to Paul to be a great man of God in God's eyes. It was the love of God that compelled the Apostle Paul to press for the prize of the high calling of Jesus Christ (Philippians 3:14).

CHAPTER 3

SPIRITUAL MOMENTUM

1 Samuel 17:48-49 (KJV) And it came to pass, when the Philistine arose, and came, and drew nigh to meet David, that David hastened, and ran toward the army to meet the Philistine. And David put his hand in his bag, and took thence a stone, and slang it, and smote the Philistine in his forehead, that the stone sunk into his forehead; and he fell upon his face to the earth.

The word *momentum* defined by Webster dictionary means "the strength or force that something has when it is moving." Christians should exercise moving force with Jesus in your life as a witness. Christians should move with momentum to let their light shine before men in an effort to win people to Jesus Christ. When the Holy Spirit moves with power in your life, change will happen. We can all experience momentum at different times and way in our lives. The Holy Spirit is the power and force that helps me make Jesus priority in serving Him. My life should be moving with a momentum led by the Holy Spirit to serve God in ways as the Apostle Paul and others in the five-fold ministry did (Ephesians 4:8-12).

Visualize a spaceship taking off and within minutes of reaching its full momentum to reach outer space. Many people believe that the power from one asteroid has so much power and momentum, moving from space to earth, to make contact can cause mass destruction of life. More than likely, the last thing most people are thinking about (with the exception of those working in NASA and at NORAD Space Center) is being hit and annihilated by a powerful asteroid from outer space.

Another force is obviously an atomic bomb that can be unleashed like in the historical war attack and retaliation on Hiroshima. Once the power of the explosion is unleashed, nothing can stop its deadly force. The atomic bomb has overwhelming power that causes destruction. These are all examples of objects moving or operating at high momentum.

Can you visualize the power of a spaceship, 747 aircraft or a missile—in full momentum? Nothing can stop it because of the power and momentum within and behind it! This is the kind of momentum and power Jesus is looking for in Christians as they serve and witness for Him throughout the world. Saints, you have Jesus as the power inside of you. We should have a momentum in our relationship with Jesus Christ. If we do, we are connected to the Father, Son and the Holy Spirit. Therefore, your momentum is unstoppable.

I watched a movie where the stealth had a specific mission to destroy top enemy inside of a secret camp in another country's territory. As long as a trained operator is inside and leadership is on point with accuracy of targets, this multi-functioning machine can do almost anything,. The pilot engaged this stealth-fighting power in full momentum at his target with an explosive and unstoppable stealth speed. It dove down into enemy territory to a level no one could have imagined and took out the target with ease and precision in the darkness and bad conditions.

Christians have the power of Jesus Christ to engage all enemies against your and your family. God's Word tells that if we put on the whole armor of God, we can stand against the enemy. We can engage him using the armor of God. The Lord provides all that we need to stand against enemy attacks, then take him out (Ephesians 6).

Men can use this stealth fighting machine because God allows us to fight for freedom and maintain our freedom and independence. Man has the intelligence to create technology and be heroic at the same time.

Some of the highest most sophisticated trains carry high

momentum.

If a train needs to stop because a vehicle is stuck on the tracks, the momentum of that train is so forceful and powerful, that the conductor is unable to stop the train in time. I have seen at least three movies with runaway trains. Trains are not bad. Train conductors just need to know how to operate it in full power and shut down. If a truck or vehicle try to outrun a train, it is super dangerous because it will not be able to stop, and will destroy anything in the path. This is the exact same momentum Christians should exercise.

MOMENTUM MAN

AT WORK!

1 Samuel 17:40 Then he took his staff in his hand, chose five smooth stones from the stream, put them in the pouch of his shepherd's bag and, with his sling in his hand, approached the Philistine.

One of the most memorable examples of momentum in Scripture is found in the story of David and Goliath. David, a young boy was on the frontline against a giant who placed fear into the souls of King Saul's men. One small stone from a shepherd boy's bag used in a slingshot had enough force to penetrate the giant and kill him! The momentum came from this young boy trusting in his

God and God's power behind and through the stone, ultimately defeating the giant. David was prepared to take out the enemy with his five stones, but all he needed was one stone to slay Goliath.

I believe God put the exact momentum in that stone needed to take Goliath down. It is amazing when you see God take your giants out! When I was growing up, one stone would only leave a huge knot on the forehead. Nevertheless, God used this ordinary stone in a different way. This stone was specifically used under the control of God through David.

I believe God is in the business of making men with the heart of King David. David was a man after God's own heart.

In one of the Marvel Comics movies, Iron Man saved the day when a nuclear missile was released to destroy the city. He used full momentum and power from within his heart piece and suit to catch that missile midair and redirect it into a black hole within an enemy's operation cell. This enemy had been constantly releasing multiple demon-like creatures by the hundreds throughout the world. It was an ugly scene that made me think about the tribulation on earth. I am glad that I will be raptured and be with Jesus (1Thessalonians 4).

It was Iron Man's love for humanity that propelled him to fight and save the world. Sometimes when you fight, you are saving more people than you can imagine! Put on the whole armor of God, which is your iron man suit, and take a stand against all enemy attacks (Ephesians 6). Put on your iron man suit and save some lives.

I cannot leave out The Incredible Hulk, who is also one of my favorite heroic characters. One incident with gamma rays changed his life to become perhaps the strongest creature on Earth whenever someone makes him mad. When the enemy makes the character, David Banner angry, he becomes the Incredible Hulk. The Incredible Hulk moves with strength and momentum that is far greater than army tanks, helicopters, missiles and ships. His strength seems to have no measure.

If the enemy makes you mad, you need to get a Hulk-like attitude in the spirit and fight back! We need an incredible transformation in our hearts and spirits. We also need a spiritual momentum in our lives to serve God and to stand against all enemies and principalities. Here is my new Marvel Comics character, the newest Avenger, "Momentum Man." He has a cape and more strength and power than Superman, Iron Man and The Incredible Hulk!

When track stars race in the Olympics, they run with speed that has an unstoppable momentum and force in their strides toward the finish line for first place. Think of the power in the mind flowing to the limbs to push for more momentum to win the race. This momentum is different in every Olympic event.

We put momentum in so many different things in life. You can think about just about everything in the world that people put momentum in. To get a college degree, people put extra effort and momentum into each specific course to complete the degree. To be a movie star, actors put extra effort and momentum (force) in getting that star role. Many people put in extra effort, sacrifice and commitment to be the best athlete, star in Hollywood, gambler or gang member.

Be careful with your momentum you put into a relationship with someone you're not married to. You might be going full force and too fast when the relationship might not be real! Make sure it's real before you put everything in it.

Our momentum must be prioritized and pleasing to God. We need to make sure we do things with high morals and ethics before the eyes of God. The Apostle Paul must be one of the greatest examples in the Bible and in life after Jesus converted him. He put all his momentum into the demonstration and witness of serving our Lord, Jesus Christ.

There is a movie called "Unstoppable" where personnel were assigned to stop this moving train to avoid a catastrophe. Nevertheless, only God can control and stop any momentum and any force. His power is greater than all things. However, the devil has momentum also. Satan's momentum is directed towards destroying your life. He tries to make you believe that God does not love you. Satan puts force into his efforts to break up marriages and put people in bondage. He comes to kill, steal, and destroy, Jesus comes to give life and more abundantly (John 10:10). That's his momentum! He wants your life destroyed at all costs. You have a savior who has all power in His hand—Jesus Christ, who is King of Kings and Lord of Lords!

When God is in action, His momentum is superior and greater than all forces in the universe, above and beneath the earth. God's power and momentum overcome all things. The enemy must release his grip on your life because Jesus said loose him and set him free! Jesus can rescue anyone at any time in life. Try Jesus now!

God is the one who can lift you up when momentum of suicide tries to overtake you. When momentum of depression and the momentum of anything else try to steal and wreck your life, you need to call on the Lord Jesus Christ for strength to overcome it. God's power is used to rescue your life and anyone else's life. God's power can deliver you from desires to commit adultery, fornicate and indulge in pornography with multiple partners, hating, and all other ungodly, evil things.

There is no momentum of the devil that's too hard for God. God can make things come to a screeching halt! You could have been under witchcraft, voodoo, psychics, false prophets, wrong doctrine, living a lie in marriage, homosexuality, pornography, prostitution and adultery for years, and the devil thinks his momentum is still moving at a steady pace in your life. But God steps in and stops that devil in his tracks.

God wants you to know that you have an advocate, the Holy Spirit (John 16). There is nothing in life that has so much momentum (force and power) that God can't handle it. Turn to God for help and worship Him. God never fails. His power exceeds everybody's momentum and all the tricks and lies of the enemy. God is unstoppable! Get on God's side!

Do not allow the enemy to trap you or trick you into being consumed by ungodly things. Keep your mind on Jesus so temptations, depression and suicidal thoughts do not enter your mind!

You have power inside of you that makes you a spiritual momentum man. This power is given by the Holy Spirit. You have the word of God that has more power and force within it than all weapons on earth and all the enemy's devices and power. God wants you to use the momentous power in the spirit that He has granted you. No weapon formed against you shall prosper (Isaiah

54:17). Put on the whole armor of God and stand against all enemies (Ephesians 6:11). You are God's momentum man and every enemy will flee by God's power. God gets results through His word and power.

BELIEVE IN JESUS CHRIST

John 20:27-29 Then He said to Thomas, reach your finger here, and look at my hands; And reach your hand here, and put it into my side. Do not be unbelieving, but believing, And Thomas answered and said to Him, My Lord, and My God! Jesus said Thomas because you have seen Me, you have believed. Blessed are those who have not seen and yet believed.

Merriam-Webster Dictionary defines *believe* as "to accept or regard (something) as true." Another definition means to accept as true and honest, genuine or real. One example is when you believe in the Scriptures and how it transforms your life. Another personal example is with your parents. A father and mother are the two key people children believe in the most throughout their childhood until they meet Jesus as Lord. This kind of believing stems from knowing and having expectation of being nurtured and cared for by your parents. We automatically believed each day that our father would go to work and pay all bills. You believed that you had no worries in your father providing food for his family. We also believe automatically that mother was going to prepare dinner each night and provide exactly what we needed to live and be sustained in life growing up.

The good news is that Jesus is our sustainer and provider of life. Jesus has compassion for all people, believers and non-believers. We know it because of His love, grace and mercy for all people. He continues to open His arms for everyone to receive His love.

Today, there is an abundance of religions that people flock to without any research and in a sense of blindness and desperation. The purpose of this passage is to point everyone to the word of God to learn of Jesus Christ. Religions baffle the minds in people. The danger is that people can be lowered into false religions that do not have the only true and wise God.

Let's be clear and upfront: There is *no other* God but the God of the Holy Bible, the God who is the Father of Jesus Christ. Religions such as Buddhism, Islam, Hinduism, Paganism, Atheism, Hare Krishna, and Scientology do not worship the God of the Holy Bible. Those are false religions. Whatever you believe in is what you will trust and walk in, even if it's wrong. You will probably die for it.

Jim Jones was a false preacher who led hundreds to their death because they believed in him. David Koresh led people in Waco, Texas to their death because they believed and obeyed him. They did not even know Jesus Christ. He was teaching them that he was

"Jesus." If you are in a religion outside of knowing Jesus as your Lord and Savior, run as fast as you can. These religions do not have Jesus as the Son of God or as the center of their lives. They do not recognize Him as the truth, the way and the life (John 14:6).

Your belief directs and influences your life. If you believe in Jesus as your Lord and Savior, and trust Him to lead and guide you through the power of the Holy Spirit, then it will be so (John 15, 16). If you are in a religion out of Christianity, you are walking in darkness. The devil has a hold on you and I pray right now that the enemy's grip is off of you in the name of Jesus Christ, the Son of the living God. Become a believer today while it is not too late! Become a believer because God has took the enemy's grip off of your life.

Several times throughout Scripture, Jesus touched people in different situations. What was so important about His touch? Jesus always made it personal and those He touched believed in His healing power. Healing was the result of Jesus' touch.! It was His love that restored us. He touched our lives so that we could believe and be focused on Him. He touched the blind, He touched the lame, He touched those with leprosy; He touched those who were demon possessed and those who were tortured by demonic spirit. Jesus even touched the dead and called them back to life.

He allowed the hem of His garment to be touched by a woman with a blood issue, so she could be healed. Jesus never turns us away from His love. His unfailing love, grace, mercy, and healing power are available to everyone. Jesus can touch your life today if you believe it

The blind man wanted to see and finally found the one who could change the course of his life (John 9). When you ask the Lord about seeing, trust Him. Your old spiritual scales will fall off and your eyes will be opened (Acts 9).

The woman with the issue of blood just wanted to touch the hem of His garment. Jesus asked, "Who touched me?" When she confessed, He spoke to her, saying, "Your faith has made you whole." God wants us to have that kind of faith, knowing that He will make us whole (Luke 8:43-47). Even if the physicians can not heal you, the Lord will make you whole again. You just need to ask Him to touch your situation, no matter what it is; He has the power to change it. You must believe.

Questions and Discussion:

1. What was Thomas' issue? _____

2. Why is believing so important in Scripture?
_____

3. Do you have a problem like Thomas did?

MARRIAGE

BONE OF MY BONES

GENESIS 3:23-24 And Adam said: This is now bone of my bones and flesh of my flesh; She shall be called Woman, because she was taken out of Man. Therefore, a man shall leave his father and mother and be joined to his wife, and they shall become one flesh.

George Robertson was a highly regarded, well-known atheist in his community. There was nothing you could do to make George change his mind to believe that Jesus is the Son of God. His primary focus was the Big Bang Theory. In his mind, God does not exist! He was too foolish to believe in the right thing. The atheists have different excuses much like the average nonbeliever. George Robertson's lovely wife and soul mate was Mrs. Deloris Robertson. She was diagnosed with cancer and both saw the X-rays results taken by Dr. Maurice Doolittle. George broke down and cried when he saw the results. After the doctor stated that she had only a few months to live, George went home and cried throughout the night.

George was hard as nails until the doctor's report came. He realized what he was about to lose. George had to nurture his wife. However, Deloris was a Christian who could not resist telling her husband daily who she was. Deloris visited with her pastor, praying and believing that the cancer was gone. She spoke words of declaration over her own life.

After walking inside of her prayer closet, about three days of observing and listening to her pray to God in Jesus name, something changed in him. George asked his wife if she truly believed in God. "Just as much as we are married, I love God even more," she replied. He loved his wife so much, that he would do almost anything to make her happy.

They went back to the hospital after three weeks of praying. This time, the X-ray had no images of cancer inside her brain and breast. George had heard his wife mention several Scriptures that spoke of Jesus healing people. This was the best day of his life!

"Thank you, Jesus!" George shouted. George went home with Deloris and he went into her prayer closet. He asked Jesus to come into his heart. He thanked God for saving his wife's life. She is his soul mate for over 35 years of marriage.

He went to church that Sunday with her, accepted Jesus publicly before the church and testified of God's goodness to his wife and himself. He told the congregation that he knows that Jesus is real because He saved his wife and that he saved him from being alone without her! "God is good," said George. After seeing what God did for them, George is no longer an atheist. George is now a newborn Christian. He was so thankful to realize that is was God who gave him a soul mate.

Make no mistake about God ordaining marriages between man and woman. He establishes the perfect picture of soul mates in union. This is one of the most recognized pictures of seeing love in action on earth. A soul mate is the perfect friend and intimate partner in your love life. This union is the perfect relationship if God is in it. This person is extremely close to you and knows your heart to a certain extent.

It is vitally important to know that man was not meant to be alone. That's why God designed a helpmeet for him. He needs all her help! In Scripture, the "bone" is powerful in its meaning. The bone signifies structure and support from the woman to her husband. She must support him and stand by his side. The bone has nutrients, strength and power. She is the helpmeet and bone that keeps him standing in power so he can serve in ministry and the home. The woman was created with love inside of her, specifically created to please God and her husband. She was created to help him using her love.

Adam saw her and called her, "bone of my bones and flesh of my flesh." There was an immediate, intensely high level of attraction and desire with love, affection and intimacy when he saw her. I believe Adam's internal chemistry was boiling in the overflow because he knew this gift was from God. It is powerful when you know God gave you a woman!

Life was perfect when he saw her. She was flawless from head to toe, a perfect God-sent queen! No goddess could compare to this woman! The wife is sent by God to be strong and supportive to her husband. She was handmade by God!

The woman was pleased as well that she had a man (a king and priest from God) to honor, reverence and respect, as well as love. She belongs to someone who she can give her love to. Nevertheless, the woman was made for man, not man for the woman. Therefore, keep the order that God established. Adam and Eve became soul mates for life and nothing was to come between them. Soul mate simply means having an inner spiritual connection that ties a man and woman together with love. They are fully aware of each other's love and are in love. Nothing breaks this bond between the couple and Jesus is the bonding in the marriage.

WE ARE ONE IN JESUS CHRIST!

God ordained marriage between man and woman to produce children as man and wife. God instituted marriage and no one can break it. The other marriage is between Christ and His Church, His Saints (Revelation 19).

These are the only marriages blessed by God Himself in accordance with Genesis 3:23-24 and Mark 10:6-9. God does not want man to drift into the mindset of people as described in Romans 1:18-32.

When people fall or step out of true matrimony, they open the gates for demons to enter their lives. The enemy feeds off the weaknesses and wickedness of people. They fall for anything the enemy throws at them such as adultery and vindictive actions and thinking. The enemy makes sin look and feel good, then distorts the mind and spirit to make people believe that whatever the sin is, it's okay.

Sin is a trap from the devil. His job is to lower you back in the "world of anything goes." You must understand that the enemy is the author of lies, confusion and evil. He wants to destroy your blessed marriage. Keep your vows that you vowed to live by. Love each other with the fullness of love and passion. Jesus is the strength and power cord in your marriage! Do not cut it with acts of disobedience.

Keep your marriage in prayer and before God always. The adversary roams as a roaring lion, seeking whom he may devour.

God will bless you and change your situation. You do not have to allow your marriage and yourself to fall victim to the enemy. Instead, walk in the victory daily! You deserve to be blessed by God. Those who love the Lord are praying for all people to be blessed by God's true marriage principles. The love of Jesus Christ connects husband and wife and leaves out all potential threats.

Questions & Discussion:

1. Why was woman taken out of man? _____

2. Why must he leave mother and father and join to his wife?

_____

_____

3. Why is she called "bone of my bones" in Scripture?

_____

SPEAK WELL OF YOUR HUSBAND

2 Samuel 6:23 Therefore Michal the daughter of Saul had no child unto the day of her death.

In the sixth chapter of the second book of Samuel, when the ark of God was recovered, King David danced for God in an attitude of worship. The Scripture says that he "danced before the LORD with all his might" (2 Samuel 6:14). He really did not care what the public had to say. This is a great sign of surrendering to complete worship, regardless of who is around you and what they think. The message in worship is to open your heart to God and let Him know you worship Him in spirit and truth.

When Michal, King David's wife, saw him dancing, she despised him in her heart and confronted him (2 Samuel 6:16, 20). She put her mouth on a man after God's own heart! And as a result, Michal ended up barren until her death.

Wives, speak to your husband in the most honorable way from your lips and heart. One of the most important things a woman can say to her husband is, *I believe in you!* When you speak that kind encouragement to your husband, he'll feel like your "Superman." Speak well to your husband. Do not allow any form of poison from your tongue, lips and thoughts. Proverbs 4 tells us to speak life into him. Likewise, the husband should speak life into her. When you come together as husband and wife in obedience to God, something good will always happen because of His goodness toward you. Therefore, expect the Lord to pour out blessings so that your wife will be fruitful to the glory of God

CHAPTER 4

UNEQUALLY YOKED

2 Corinthians 6:14 Be ye not unequally yoked together with unbelievers: for what fellowship hath righteousness with unrighteousness? And what communion hath light with darkness?

When it comes to relationships, the Apostle Paul makes it clear to the believer where he or she should stand with an unbeliever. The Bible simply tells us not to be unequally yoked. When two hearts agree in Jesus Christ, they are yoked in the spirit because they are born-again believers. A strong covenant relationship can exist. A man who is a non-believer engages in a relationship with a Christian woman will not be equally yoked.

The first chapter of Romans talks about relationship that should never exist The Bible is clear; a marriage consisting of one man and one woman together is the only authorized and blessed relationship before God. Anything else is a defilement and abomination before God.

Be intentional about winning souls and pulling people out of a bad, demonic situation. The following is a scenario of a bad situation.

A young girl in church was deeply involved in Sunday school, church worship services, and even helping in the child care center at church. One day, she met a seemingly nice young man in church whom she was attracted to. She thought he was "Prince Charming." She ended up going out one night with him to celebrate a birthday. Later, she realized that he wanted to party every weekend after the first few months of meeting. She caved in and went to the club with him.

One night, he got high on cocaine and ecstasy. To please him, she engaged in cocaine. Later that night, he raped her and beat her, leaving her for dead in an alley behind a night club. All she had on was a towel which was wrapped around her bottom part of the body. She was left unconscious.

Lakisha survived this beating. It was a blessing that a Christian woman picked her up and took her to the hospital. There were no charges filed against her attacker because she did not know his real identity or anything about him.

Today Lakisha has broken from that side of life. She went to college and received her PhD in Forensic Psychology. She still serves in the church and worship services. She has started her own successful business where she counsels young ladies and families dealing with domestic violence, abuse and rape. God is in the middle of the healing and restoring process.

The moral of the story: Don't get involved with first appearance and someone who has nothing to do with Jesus in their lives. When you see trouble brewing, run!

The problem with an unequally relationship such as the one in the scenario is that one person has the love of God inside their heart and the other person does not. That means something else resides in their heart. They are guided by something else, and usually that would be a dark spirit. The dark spirit will cause real problems in this undeveloped relationship. You will find yourself in fights, disputes, hatred and jealousy because you are not equally yoked. There will always be ongoing fights until someone makes a desperate cry to get out of this awful, evil relationship.

Either one of you know Jesus as Lord and Savior, the other person is in a dark spiritual point in their life. The Bible does not condone abuse, nor does it tell you that you must remain in an abusive relationship. God does want you to get help and get out of it using common sense and prayer.

Ephesians is a strong standard for what a relationship should be like, especially in a marriage. You must read and apply the word of God as the authority in all situations. Also, use common sense as

God gave you. His word is your initial and final authority for all things. We all have a sense of discernment; therefore, you can easily detect that one of them have a relationship with God and the other one does not. God does not share love with a dark spirit. One or the other must dwell inside your heart.

The deception comes when a woman thinks it's honorable to have a baby with a man who lives in darkness and rejects Jesus. She does not realize the depth of this trap by Satan. In her mind, she thinks she can change him with her strategy. However, only God can change a man who lives in darkness.

Ask questions and learn about the person you are attracted to. Make sure this person is satisfying in God's sight before you make any commitment or get intimate with him or her.

Being unequally yoked can exist in any age group. Teenagers are prime targets for engaging in the wrong type of relationships; however, adults aren't exempt. Teens, don't give yourselves up sexually to become popular in school. Don't do anything as adults to impress your friend. This might mean you are in lust rather than serious about relationship. This is not to condemn you; this was written to protect you from pregnancy and STDs.

The spirit behind an unequally yoked relationship is to undermine your walk with the Lord. God wants you to be obedient for the good of your life. He wants you to have the blessed life. Yoke with someone that God sends your way and you'll know it for sure.

Questions & Discussion:

1. What does this passage in 2 Corinthians mean to you as husband/wife?

   _____
   _____

2. What actions would you take to comply with 2 Corinthians 6?

   _____
   _____
   _____

VICTORY IN JESUS CHRIST

1 Corinthians 15:57 But thanks be to God, which giveth us the victory through our Lord Jesus Christ.

As Christians, we are victorious, no matter what kind of hardship comes our way. We are more than conquerors through Jesus Christ. Every Christian must adapt the mindset of being victorious in Jesus Christ. We place our lives in the hand of Jesus Christ and Jesus gives us the victory. The blood covers all sin. The blood makes us victorious in Jesus Christ.

We do not worship a governmental system or rules and laws of a country. We do not worship politics nor attach ourselves to a personal political party as our identity. We abide by Romans 13. Every governing official must align themselves with the Word of God. We do not base our lives on any government ideology and political parties. We do not allow an ideology to form in our hearts and minds or alter our behavior and attitude. Christians base their beliefs on the spirit of truth and honor in Jesus Christ! Christians follow Jesus Christ (Matthew 16:24-25) (Matthew 22:36-38).

If Christians are involved in politics, they should be about 100% solid truth and honor for the best of humanity and equality. Everything should be in aligned with Jesus Christ, but there is too much contradiction, corruption and division rather than the Christian lifestyle. We should not attach ourselves to any demonic influences. As Christians, our victory is in the blood of Jesus Christ, who died on the cross for the sins of the world and saved us from God's wrath. I am so glad that God opened my eyes to see who I belong to and my identity, which is in Jesus Christ.

When you know that you are a true Christian, life takes on a new meaning. I am of the Christian party. The Christian party is a group of believers who have accepted Jesus Christ in their hearts and follow Him only. I am not of these political parties that divide people because they have taken the personal identity of a political system.

The Christian is free in Jesus Christ. God is real and you know it. Love and peace are the objectives. Stop the division. It's about expressing love over hate. Love is more powerful than anyone. Love is the power source that eliminates all manner of evil in your life. God can restore.

This is the same God who restored Nineveh. He sent Jonah to preach repentance and the city was restored. America with its deeply-rooted racial issues need prayer and the Holy Spirit. America needs to be set free.

If you have ever been dedicated to anything in your life, you need to be dedicated to making a change for the world to love each other like Jesus. Americans are at a breaking point that will result in a catastrophe if nothing is done to remove hate from the entire government and people. Motivation and commitment to doing the right thing, along with self- determination can turn things around for the better. It can change people who dwell in negative environments to adapt an attitude of love in Jesus Christ. Victory is in Jesus Christ (1 Corinthians 15; 1 John 5:4-5). Hate and racism comes from the pits of hell—the devil himself. Love and kindness comes from Jesus Christ, directly from heaven. Our victory is in Jesus' name! All demons flee and tremble at the name of Jesus! This division can be destroyed by demonstrating the power of love in Jesus Christ, who gives a change of heart from evil to good. Good outweighs evils! Good overcomes evil! (Romans 12:20). Bringing people together for the common good must be a priority in the world. Children are watching you and being molded into what you are. Set the example in love through Jesus Christ.

If you have the audacity to get into the choir, praise team, sit in the pews, or stand in the pulpit, then proclaim God's word of peace, joy, love and forgiveness and everything that God can do for people. God is also able to stop the division.

You have a responsibility to your children and their children to build godly, spiritual morality. Proverbs 22:6 says, "Train up a child in the way he should go: and when he is old, he will not depart from it." If you train them up in the love of God, they will remain forever in the love of God. However, if you do the opposite and train them in hate and racism they'll become as Satan's tools to cause evil on the earth, just as demons do today (Mark 5). Love is the only solution for hate and bigotry. Love can literally eradicate hate, bigotry and all forms of evil. Read what God did and offered us in John 3:16.

If you are a Christian, it is your duty and obligation to take a firm stance and get results. Stop the division between whites and blacks and every race on this planet! Stop profiling due to racial disparage. If you have not done anything but stand in your pulpit and fellowship with people within your race because you are comfortable, you may want to check your heart! Stop the division!

In a world filled with blessings, no one should have to form "Black Lives Matter" to get attention and start a movement. Stop the division! No one should take babies from their mothers, having to nurse them on borders to prove a point of political policies. Stop the division.

Christians must stand up boldly in God's righteousness against Satan's tool of racism. Racism divides and destroys people all around the world. People are God's creation. God loves every person He created. It's not a color or race thing in God's eyes. All men are created equal. There is no superior race! There is no superior person! Please ask God to erase it out of your mind if you are thinking that! This kind of thought sparks evil. All men are created equal. Read the first five chapters of the Book of Genesis. You will see that God never placed several different men in the Garden of Eden with different races. God placed only one man in the garden in His image and named him, Adam (Genesis 1:27).

Church, stand up and bring peace! Come together and bond in

unity. God did not make a white church, black church, Asian church, Hispanic church. The church, although diverse in culture, is *one church* because Jesus Christ is the head (Colossians 1:17-18).

As far as I can remember, this division of race has been before the 1920s up to now. This demonic influence plans to remain in each family that displays racism so that their children will be the same. Jesus wants the opposite; He wants loving, respectable, kindhearted, honorable children.

Division reveals the adversary, Satan, who attacks at all times because no one is truly working together. People give the enemy a victory shout when they allow him to spread evil! Instead, we are supposed to be giving Jesus Christ the permanent and highest praise, worship and victory shout! We have the victory in Jesus Christ, no matter what it looks like. According to Ephesians 4:5 there is only "one Lord, one faith, one baptism." No one is higher than God! Certainly, no government, king, queen or president has any measure toward God. They must all bow before the almighty living God, Jesus Christ!

THE GREATEST LOVE!

John 15:13 Greater love has no one than this: to lay down one's life for one's friends.

Jesus makes it clear that He will lay down His life for all mankind. Then He makes a profound statement about laying life down for a friend. Jesus not only calls us His children, calls us _friend._

Friends don't leave friends hanging. Friends do what is needed to help a friend survive. Friends stick closer than a brother. Friends have an "I have your back attitude." Jesus has your back more than any other person. Jesus is the kind of friend that you can count on. He will not give up on you.

In the movie, *Tombstone,* Doc Holiday was Wyatt Earp's best friend. It took Doc Holiday make Wyatt Earp realize that he was not fast enough for their enemy. Although Doc Holiday was on his sick bed, close to death, he managed to get up and take the place of his friend in a gunfight that would have otherwise taken Wyatt's life. It's powerful to have a best friend like that!

Doc Holiday went to the meet out point in which Wyatt was called out to (under a tree) by the enemy, Johnny Ringo. When the gunman realized it was Doc Holiday, all the hot air and noise dissipated because he was in shock! Doc Holiday said, "I am here.." Johnny Ringo's response was, "The fight is not with you" Doc Holiday said, "It is because we did not get to finish it." Johnny Ringo in fear responds "I was just playing." Doc Holiday said to him, "I wasn't!" They drew their pistols and of course, Doc Holiday drew his pistol much faster! Johnny Ringo went down under that tree.

The point is not about killing. The point is that a friend stood in when he knew that his friend was going to be killed by this villain. Doc Holiday stood up in a moment of crisis. He even got off his sickbed to help his friend.

Please understand that this was not written for you to get revenge by using any means of violence. This western movie was used as an example to depict how a friend stood up for another friend. In our lives, Jesus stands up for us every time a demon attacks. Jesus stands up every time trouble comes our way. Every time the devil thinks he has a grip on our lives, Jesus makes the enemy release us and we come out with victory in Jesus' name. If Jesus did not use His power for our sake, demons would be unleashed to destroy us. Thank God for His mercy and power of protection. Thank God for the Love of Jesus Christ on our side.

There are other people who stood up for people and became a friend to America. If I had to give an example of a perfect model other than Jesus, it would be Dr. Martin Luther King, Jr. Dr. King's character and spiritual belief employed to help all people and break down color barriers and racism. He stood for Jesus Christ. No one in their right mind would have come up with a non-violent strategy of the *March on Washington, August 28, 1963*. This historic event not only put a halt and a dent in the severity of racism, but it united people in ways no one else has ever done. Dr. King was on mission. God sent this African-American man of God, as a "Moses" to deliver his people from racism, injustice and inequality. Yes, much like God's people who were under Pharaoh in Egypt, African Americans were suffering from severe racism. It takes people who love God to recognize that God has a greater love for him. It takes someone who is willing to lay down His life for a friend.

A FATHER'S LOVE

Exodus 20:12 Honor your father and your mother, so that you may live long in the land the Lord your God is giving you.

Our family always honored my father and mother. When I think about love, I think about the godly love my parents displayed to their children. The sheer love of them taking care of me as a child is a blessing. Love is powerful, and it flows from the parents to their children. Most of the time, children miss it or take it for granted until they grow up. God wants them to remember Ephesians 6:2: "Honor thy father and mother." My father loved his family and spent real quality time with us. He taught us valuable lessons—honor our mother, work ethics, be disciplined, respect others, and much more. We were happy when he also played basketball and football with the boys. At times, he would even race us in the yard. It was exciting to see his competitive side after hard day's work. It is a blessed feeling to remember those days of growing up under my father's covering and protection.

The goodness of God comes to my mind immediately when I think of my biological father, Joe Arthur Doyle. The goodness ignites my heart because he is my father and how he treated us with dignity, respect, love and care. When I needed surgery and was in need of blood, my father gave his blood. He never complained nor mentioned it. It was just a fatherly thing to give a part of himself to his son, much like Jesus gave His blood for us.

My father was a hero and a man of honor! He served not only his family, but in the United States Army during the Korean War, where he achieved multiple Bronze Star Medals. Throughout almost 40 years of construction work, my father worked in hot and cold weather, even on days when he was sick or didn't feel well. He provided for his family. No matter what, food was on the table and we had the best clothes. My father, Joe Arthur Doyle, is indeed the best man I know in my heart. I know it because Jesus put it there in my heart. There's nothing like knowing that your father loves you more than you know, even when words sometimes don't flow. It's just a man thing! We just know that Dad loves us so much. My father is my hero. I could never be where I am if it wasn't for him. He was our father, protector, provider, and the priest of his house. He's my father, blessed by

God to bless his sons and daughters, and his wife. I thank God that he had me. I'm able to preach the gospel because of his love and support.

So, I want to leave this note for his grandchildren, and for generations to come. God blessed a father to bless his family and as a result, he produced a preacher of the Gospel for God's glory, in Jesus' name.

Questions & Discussion:

1. What does it mean to honor your father and mother? _____
_____

2. What New Testament book speaks of honoring father and mother? _____

3. Do you have honor in your heart? _____

4. Why is honoring parents significant?

LOVE IMPACTS!

Luke 6:35 But love your enemies, do good to them, and lend to them without expecting to get anything back. Then your reward will be great, and you will be children of the Highest, because he is kind to the ungrateful and wicked.

Love impacts all people, including your enemies. The effects are really strong and powerful. In fact, love is the greatest weapon against all enemies. The Apostle Paul (formerly known as Saul), was an enemy to God. He hated Christians. Look at the conversion that God brought upon him. The co-worker that is always on your back, monitoring your every move, talking negative about you, and trying desperately to get you fired, don't have anything on you. In fact, because of your love, the reverse may happen to her or him. They just might be forced to resign. Nevertheless, love does not wish badly on anyone. Remember this, don't let them get the best of you. God can fight all our battles.

An enemy is one of the worst things anyone can have especially when you can identify a person as an enemy. Enemies come in different packages, bodies, and in spirit form. God deals with that enemy on various fronts. In Luke 6:35, the Lord is referring to our earthly enemies. He is talking about people who could possibly have a form of hatred toward you.

When Cain slew Abel, his brother was not the enemy. He did it out of a jealous spirit and a dominating spirit of disobedience. When you display love, you are in line with God. Instead, Cain was displaying evil and hate. Nevertheless, his brother Abel was not the enemy. Cain formulated in his mind that his brother was the enemy and that fostered evil to kill. Cain did not realize how his actions affected his family and generations to come. The actions of Cain still affect us.

We must bless everybody we can, especially our brothers, sisters and our neighbors. Your family is not the enemy. Don't allow the devil to twist your mind into hating your family members. It does not take much for one family member to spark something, only for the enemy to run with it. You might have one controlling family member controlling and with a huge mouth! The same family is loving and kind. Don't allow what you think of them and their behavior cause them to be an enemy. Tell the devil that he is a liar and go back to the depths of hell. Tell your family members that you love them right now

God tells us to do good—even to a bully. The bully's heart can also be changed. Take someone with you to witness and keep the peace so the devil will not interfere.

Another technique to blessing your enemies is to bless them secretly with a present or surprise. Purchase their lunch or send them a Christian movie or CD. Give them a nice card with an inspirational scripture.

God is showing us that we should not destroy people with violence and with the tongue by using profane language! It gets us nowhere. It only makes things worse.

You need to become a peacemaker to disseminate love in the environment (Matthew 5:9). Foster a different environment and atmosphere by praying, praising God and worshipping Him. In doing this, your presence will positively impact all your enemies. Prayer and praise can change the enemy's heart. Maintain a godly attitude and behavior.

THE POWER OF LOVE HEALS

Acts 14:8-10 And there sat a certain man at Lystra, impotent in his feet, being a cripple from his mother's womb, who never had walked: The same heard Paul speak: who steadfastly beholding him, and perceiving that he had faith to be healed, Said with a loud voice, Stand upright on thy feet. And he leaped and walked.

In Acts 14, the Apostle Paul heals an impotent man from birth by the power of the Holy Spirit. The impotent man is used to demonstrate God's power of healing. Jesus healed so many people throughout the New Testament. Jesus has so much love and power for His people we can call upon Him anytime. His love and His power are unlimited. No one can put a cap on love or His power.

The man was impotent, which in the Greek means *adunatos*. Adunatos means a person is unable and powerless. This person is ineffective, helpless and incapable. There are areas in a person's life that make them impotent. When you discover your impotent area, call on Jesus to revitalize and make you whole.

The Apostle could only heal this man through the love and power of Jesus Christ in faith. All the glory goes to the Son of God! It is important that faith exists in order for miracles and healings to manifest. Jesus healed a crippled man in Matthew 9. It is the power of his love that heals and delivers every person. Whatever you are going through or have gone through, Jesus can heal you!

In John 5, Jesus healed a lame man who was lying at the gate by the pool of Bethesda for 38 years. Jesus knew all about him. In fact, Jesus asked him if he wanted to be made well. In verse eight, Jesus told the man to pick up his mat and walk, and he did so. He was healed. We must understand that it is sheer miraculous power and authority that come from Jesus Christ when He speaks. Please understand that all power is in His hands.

Love overshadows all things because it's in Jesus Christ! Jesus' love has maximum power to heal any circumstance. Jesus' love and power conquers all, according to His will. There are people who need healing from the listed conditions in Galatians 5:19-21: "The acts of the flesh are obvious: sexual immorality, impurity and debauchery; idolatry and witchcraft; hatred, discord, jealousy, fits of rage, selfish ambition, dissensions, factions and envy; drunkenness, orgies, and the like. I warn you, as I did before, that those who live like this will not inherit the kingdom of God."

One primary behavior that cripples people is the act of adultery. Another one that people are blind to is idol worship. Idol worship will cripple you and you will not know it until it's preached to you on Sunday morning at church. There's such a lack of concern for one another. It's an epidemic in America and around the world. Adultery is a painful and evil act against the partner in marriage. Sadly, it's more of a norm. Adultery strikes and impacts right at the heart. It also destroys and cripples a person in spirit and soul. The only way to recover is through the power of love and forgiveness received from Jesus Christ. I want you to know that God can heal you from that trauma at any time.

The way to avoid any of this is to love each other as Christ loved the church. Love your husband and reverence him as the head of the house and walk as one in marriage (Ephesians 5:22-25). If you submit to God's way, you will not commit adultery. God's love has all the power in it. God's love is the seed that you need so you can overcome sin and grow in God.

Be a positive person and foster your positive attitude around others every day. Being positive makes you a winner and victorious. Victory is in your attitude! Victory has power inside of it when you speak it! Even your attitude has special power that can't be denied! Wake up and start your day with prayer. Keep your positive attitude so victory will be the outcome no matter what.

1 Samuel 17:50 So David triumphed over the Philistine with a sling and a stone; without a sword in his hand he struck down the Philistine and killed him.

God will give you a victory stone to defeat all enemies. You must have a godly attitude because there is a force inside of it! Goliath found out the hard way! Goliath had to fall! He underestimated God and a young boy, named David. The problem with your enemies is that they don't know the God who's on your side. Don't let any giants or anything break your positive spirit. Don't allow any giants make you run from your anointing. You are victorious in mind, body, soul and spirit! You are a child of God (1 John 3:1).

Being positive is contagious. You can spread it and fill the atmosphere with joy. You can encourage others by not allowing negative things to enter your spirit. Don't let the enemy steal your smile or joy. I had to remind myself that people need to hear positive sermons to help in their deliverance; to restore and build people up in Jesus Christ. Get rid of your giants by walking in the Spirit in Jesus. Get rid of your giants by thinking with the right attitude! Tell the enemy, "Victory is mine in Jesus Christ!" (1 Corinthians 15)

You can run the race set before you with a positive and victorious attitude. That is exactly what the Apostle Paul was speaking of when he was referring to running the race for Jesus as a witness (1 Timothy 4:7). It is your spiritual positive attitude that will win in the race (Hebrews 12). Watch how many people you impact and how many souls are won to Jesus Christ. You can do it. Start with one; if you believe in yourself like Jesus believes in you. Those things that use to weigh you down and take over your mind must fall off. You have a new man inside you with a new attitude. Put off those weights and put on God (Hebrews 12:1). A broken attitude involves traits such as hatred, jealously, envy, strife or even an evil spirit. Don't allow any of those traits to become part of your life.

The first king who was anointed by God in the Old Testament was King Saul. However, he later became disobedient and prideful to God. The prophet Samuel told him that God was going to take away his kingdom because of his disobedience (1 Samuel 7:15; 1 Samuel 13:1-14; 1 Samuel 15). God did exactly what the prophet Samuel said. King Saul also had gained a new warrior in his camp, that being David.

He was just a young boy; nevertheless, this same young boy was a giant slayer. He defeated the giant, named Goliath and many more men. David had a positive attitude. King Saul found himself growing jealous of David to the point he wanted to kill David.

David became king because the throne was turned over to him after the prophet Samuel had anointed him by God (1 Samuel 16). King Saul had died by falling on his own sword. His son, Jonathan, died also. It is always better to walk in the anointing, obeying God and remaining positive. King David's positive attitude and his heart to trust God pleased God. We should all live a positive and obedient life. Then you can watch God move with blessings in your life. He will give you the good life. Just stay positive in the Lord.

God wants us to live the good life. He wants us healthy, full of strength and joy. You may want to start smiling every chance you get! It creates a positive atmosphere. Take on King David's attitude of walking in blessings. It will help your attitude change.

One major step in life is to put off the weight and put on God. Put on God by surrendering your will to Him. Put on God by serving and becoming a dedicated witness.

Live for God! Live for you! Live for your family! Win a soul. Don't you give up on God! Your health means a lot to the Lord. He gave you this earthen vessel to take care of it—not to worship it; but to live a blessed life in Jesus Christ. If you live for anything else, you are not aligned with Jesus. If you are not taking care of yourself, you are not aligned with Jesus. When you go on a diet, imagine how you study the word of God. Use that method of training your body. At the same time, when you are fasting and praying, you will also get a breakthrough if you are vigorously doing it.

Nevertheless, it's the power of love that we desire each day. We long for that kind of love that can heal us. The power of love can turn everything around. The power of love can heal a broken heart and every area of our lives. We need to have faith in His love. Whatever you do and wherever you are, pursue God because His love never fails. His love has all power to heal and restore lives.

CHAPTER 5

LOVE FILLS GAPS!

John 20:19-21 Then, the same day at evening, being the first day of the week, when the doors were shut where the disciples were assembled, for fear of the Jews, Jesus came and stood in the midst, and said to them, "Peace be with you." When He had said this, He showed them His hands and His side. Then the disciples were glad when they saw the Lord. So, Jesus said to them again, "Peace to you! As the Father has sent Me, I also send you."

Jesus filled every gap in the world through His ministry, His death on the cross and His resurrection from the dead. Jesus bridged the gap so that we have access to the Father through Him.

Whatever love you need, Jesus has it just right for you. He filled gaps so you can access His love, His Father's love, and the love and intervention of the Holy Spirit. In fact, His love brings you through every condition that tries to hold you back from crossing over into your blessings.

You should not have any more gaps in your life. Jesus filled those gaps so you can have peace and joy. The love of God through Jesus fills the gaps that takes a person's mind from suicidal thoughts, depression, loneliness, mental attacks, sickness, grief, and the feeling of defeat. One of the biggest gaps filled was the sin nature of mankind described in the days of Adam and Noah. God filled the gap using an obedient man named, Noah and the construction of an ark.. God used him and his family to save creation and restart population. In the New Testament, Jesus was the gap filler for Adam's rebellion. Jesus was the Lamb of God slain for all sin. When deprivation step in, Jesus steps up and steps through it, over it and demolishes it by the blood. Deprivation wants man to recognize his fallen nature and become enslaved to sin. Jesus was crucified for all mankind. In Romans 5:8, the Apostle Paul says, "But God demonstrates his own love for us in this: While we were still sinners, Christ died for us." The enemy could not stop the move of God in Jesus Christ. He was full of grace and truth, power and authority from His Father, our God in heaven! If any gap opens in your life, Jesus is the gap filler! Call on His name, Jesus! Demons flee at His name!

THE ARK OF THE COVENANT AND THE MERCY SEAT

Hebrews 9:2-5 For there was a tabernacle made; the first, wherein was the candlestick, and the table, and the shewbread; which is called the sanctuary. And after the second veil, the tabernacle which is called the Holiest of all; Which had the golden censer, and the ark of the covenant overlaid round about with gold, wherein was the golden pot that had manna, and Aaron's rod that budded, and the tables of the covenant; And over it the cherubims of glory shadowing the mercy seat; of which we cannot now speak particularly.

God gives us mercy every day because He first loved us. His mercy was because of the blood of the Lamb. When I think of mercy, it brings tears to my eyes! Someone cares that much to look beyond my faults. It was mercy when God sent His only son, Jesus to die on the cross.

The blood was sprinkled on the mercy seat. The Greek word for mercy seat is *hilasterion*. In Romans 3:25, the Apostle Paul reminds us that God presented Jesus as a propitiation for our sins. You should never forget the image of Jesus on the cross, with His blood running down for every sinner of the world like me. I want to concentrate on the mercy seat.

God's mercy extends to all generations. Lamentations 3:22-23 says "It is of the Lord's mercies that we are not consumed, because his compassions fail not. Mercies are new every morning: great is thy faithfulness." The Ark of the Covenant was so precious to King David, who desired to have a dwelling place for God. There are so many things concerning the Ark of the Covenant. In 1 Samuel 3:3 and 1 Samuel 4:11, it speaks of the throne and divine presence of the Lord our God. Some might also view the tabernacle as significant as well. What I read and seen on several movies is this rectangular looking box covered in gold carried by several people on four corners using long poles.

The Ark of the Covenant, which is also known as the ark of the testimony (Exodus 25:16) looks like a chest box (Numbers 10:33). The Ark of Covenant was constructed at Mount Sinai. Inside of the Ark of the Covenant are two tablets of stone inscribed with the Ten Commandments, a jar of manna, and Aaron's rod. The Ten Commandments signify the law and God's covenant with Israel, and Aaron's rod. God was against sin then and He remains the same. The mercy seat was placed on top of the lid of the Ark of the Covenant. The mercy seat represents the Holy of Holies (Exodus 26:34) and the veil (Exodus 30:6). The presence of the Lord was manifested (Leviticus 16:2), and surrounding the mercy seat are the two cherubim with wings spread outward (Exodus 25:16-21; Hebrews 9:4-5; Exodus 25:22). The Ark of the Covenant is sacred and holy. Joshua used the Ark of the Covenant to part waters by the power of God and cross the Jordan River (Joshua 3-4). The Ark of the Covenant represents God's presence as on the throne (1 Samuel 3:3; 4:11). The word "mercy" means having compassion or forgiveness toward another person when you have the power to punish them for what they have done. God is the only one who can have true mercy to all people. God is merciful forever and ever, so give Him glory, honor and thanksgiving. Worship Him in the beauty of holiness! Lord, we thank you forever and ever. Amen.

GOD'S LEADING MAN

MOSES' BODY

JUDE 1:9 But even the archangel Michael, when he was disputing with the devil about the body of Moses, did not himself dare to condemn him for slander but said, "The Lord rebuke you!"

Moses was a servant and considered by God to be the humblest man on earth, at that time. The archangel Michael contended for the body of Moses against the devil. The archangel is one of God's highest-ranking angels. This particular angel mostly would assume reports directly to God. Therefore, this angel is powerful! The devil can't touch him!

I find it fascinating that God would view Moses' body to be so precious that He would send an angel to guard and protect it. God wanted the devil to know that Moses' body was holy, set apart for God.

Interestingly, Jude mentions Sodom and Gomorrah and how sexual immorality led to its destruction. God destroyed those towns due to its sin. God went against their lowliness and how they polluted their bodies with sexual immorality. However, Moses did not misuse his body. He used his body to serve God. Moses was one of God's greatest servants who listened and obeyed God according to the Book of Exodus. Moses led God's people to freedom from the rule of Pharaoh in Egypt. He was truly a man of God. God saw Moses as a faithful and honorable servant! Will you use your body to serve God?

God used Moses to display His supernatural power through the deliverance of His people. Think about it! Moses was used to announce to Pharaoh who God was and what God demands of him. When Pharaoh rejected God, plagues begin to occur in the palace and among Pharaoh's people. The 10 plagues that came upon Pharaoh and Egypt were supernatural acts of God. God was displaying His power. Not only was Moses chosen by God to be a man of deliverance, He displayed obedience and confidence in God's power and authority, which was pleasing to God. Moses was perhaps the only man who has seen the backside of God according to Exodus 33:18-23.

Do you please God at all or in any area of deliverance? God gave Moses a staff to use for His glory and for generations to come to know Him. Moses visited Pharaoh on one occasion. He threw the staff to the ground and it turned into a serpent. Pharaoh's magicians tried to show forth their power when they threw two staffs down and they became serpents. The problem was that God used the serpent (Moses' staff) to swallow, defeat and kill the magician's serpents. This act was supernatural, and Pharaoh's mind was boggled.

One of the greatest supernatural acts of God was when God opened the Red Sea. God responded to Moses' faith, and He rolled back the Red Sea like it was a thin sheet of paper. Dry ground appeared, allowing millions of people to walk through. Pharaoh was in heavy pursuit of the children of Israel (Exodus 14:21-22). When Pharaoh's army got inside the limits of the Red Sea, Moses put the staff down and the sea closed, drowning the entire army of Pharaoh (Exodus 14).

LOVE BROUGHT YOU OUT!

GEN 37:23 So when Joseph came to his brothers, they stripped him of his robe the richly oriented robe he was wearing. And they took him and threw him into the cistern. Now the cistern was empty; there was no water in it. So, when the Midianites merchants came by, his brothers pulled Joseph up out of the cistern and sold him for twenty shekels of silver to the Ishmaelite, who took him to Egypt.

Have you ever been in a pit—in a dark place, a place of bondage, captivity? This kind of pit can be anything that held you captive.

You could have been put in pit by the enemy or a family member. You could have placed *yourself* in the pit. Come out of the pit!

Joseph's brothers were so jealous of him that they put their own flesh and blood into a pit to die. The pit was also to test Joseph's relationship with God. People are in pits today to test their faith and identity in Jesus Christ. Keep in mind, he was not a person who cordially sinned. In fact, he was righteous in God's sight. Nevertheless, there are pits in nightclubs, alcohol, drugs, sexual abuse, prostitution, adultery and homosexuality. So, if you are in any of type of sinful pit, God can pull you out.

It was the love of God that protected Joseph when he was thrown into a pit by his own brothers. Love brought Joseph out of the pit to the palace. He went from darkness and brokenness to royalty and favor, the place he belonged. You belong in royalty and blessings. God will never leave you out of where you belong! Don't let anyone make you believe otherwise by pulling your life down with theirs.

A young man who acted like a thug pulled a young girl from church by persuading her with his slick talk of "I love you" and "You are the only one." Although she knew he was into cocaine and sleeping around, she started enjoying that type of attention even when no one else cared about that status of lifestyle.

In between your hardship, God is developing you and setting you up for a blessing that many will get blessed by. My mind immediately went to the amount of darkness and fear that Joseph may have experience initially. I imagined him being humiliated, frightened, confused and lost for a moment. I realize now through reading about Joseph that he had faith in God. He had God in his life! He believed in God and knew that the Lord would bring him through the darkness and all of his troubles.

The robe did not stop the brothers from throwing Joseph into the pit. They were fed up with the anointing on Joseph's life because of their own jealous spirits. Of course, they did not recognize God working in Joseph's life. The devil meant it for bad; however, God turned it for good.

Have you ever been around people who did not recognize the anointing on your life? You may have experienced some of what Joseph experienced. It might not be the pit, but something else like hate, slander or violence. Joseph's family missed the anointing on his life. Just because someone doesn't recognize the anointing on your life does not mean it's not there. Some people are just as cold and lost. Some people do not have a sense of direction. Therefore, they will miss the anointing on your life.

God chose Joseph for several reasons. One of the key reasons was to save Egypt and his people from dying from a famine. He also had to rescue his own family. Remember God already knows what

He is doing before we can ever think that far. Joseph's name in the Hebrew means "add and give increase." In Egypt, Joseph was given an Egyptian name, Zaphenath-paneah, since he needed to fit into Pharaoh's court and leadership (Genesis 41). Some believe his name means "God speaks and He lives." It also means "may He add and increase." Joseph also had a younger brother, Benjamin, and was blessed with two sons, Ephraim and Manasseh.

Joseph was a dreamer. God gave Joseph the ability to interpret dreams as well. Joseph's brothers thought that they had broken his spirit, when actually they pushed him into the favor of God. They did not know that by stripping him of the coat of many colors, they were setting him up for God's favor and blessings.

There is no way anyone can stop the blessings that God has in store for us. When the Lord sets something in motion, it will not be stopped by anyone or anything.

Joseph's coat represented royalty. His father gave it to him because he favored him. Joseph's coat is viewed as a coat of the rainbow, representing the covenant God made with Noah. Some see the coat as a representation of a priest. His father saw it as a gift and a blessing for his son.

When we have family situations, God does not turn His back on us. There are blessings in disguise that are on the way. The robe was a blessing and that is exactly why the enemy wanted to twist things in the family and cause jealousy. When Jesus rose from the dead, He wore a priestly robe. Jesus poured out the power to forgive. Joseph forgave his brothers. Forgiving is one of the hardest things to do, yet it's really not that complicated. It flows by the power of love.

EXALT THE LORD!

Psalm 30:1-5 I will exalt you, Lord, for you lifted me out of the depths and did not let my enemies gloat over me. Lord my God, I called to you for help, and you healed me. You, Lord, brought me up from the realm of the dead; you spared me from going down to the pit. Sing the praises of the Lord, you his faithful people; praise his holy name. For his anger lasts only a moment, but his favor lasts a lifetime; weeping may stay for the night, but rejoicing comes in the morning.

King David opens the passage with, "I will exalt you." The word exalt (egzolt) means "to raise high, to elevate in power, to exalt one to a throne, and to honor." This is a passage to help people understand how powerful God is in sparing you from going into a pit. If you went deep into a pit, it is God who delivers you out of it every time.

Joseph is a perfect example of one being thrown into pit and coming out by God's power. He was blessed in Pharaoh's palace. The problem is that most people do not realize that the devil want to put them into any pit of his choosing. Joseph, the son of Jacob trusted God in his life. One other problem is that many people need to get God into their lives. Choose God for your life today. Then exalt Him when He comes into your heart! (Romans 10:9)

It was love that lifted you and me out of the depths of the darkest pit. Even when we ourselves are the cause of going into a pit, God still brings us out with His power of love. Regardless of the location or what kind of pit it was, the Lord rescued you and did not allow your enemies to have any pleasure in destroying you.

King David understood that God was the God of victory over all enemies. When death wanted you, God said *no way!* I believe King David understood the intensity of battles and enemies all around him. Even though trouble was around, King David knew what God could do to all enemies. He may have remembered when King Saul threw a spear at him with intention to kill him out of jealousy. He also may have reflected on King Saul and his men chasing him in caves, mountains and throughout the region.

Because God is so good, He opens the psalm with, *I will exalt you Lord!* He remembered that God lifted and protected him from the hardness and extreme desire of his enemies to kill him. I believe so much that King David's troubles pushed him into praising God.

When God removes you from your enemies, none of your enemies can gloat. You have seen God working on your job with a bad supervisor who had all evil against you. You have seen enemies come out against your family and God cut them down in one way or another. Because you maintained your integrity and love for God, He blessed you and you exalted Him.

God placed a special anointing over David's life to be king and a man after God's own heart. King David had a repentant heart toward God. Even when sin hits hard, and we do wrong and feel so low, we must remember that weeping may endure for a night, but joy comes in the morning. There are times to weep. Nevertheless, joy comes and it relieves you. When God anoints you, challenges will come but God will help you get through it all! The Lord our God has the final word! We must praise Him at all times and give thanks to His Holy name!

Question and Discussion

1. What are some reasons the psalmist speaks of exalting God?

2. What is one key importance of exalting Him

FIRST LOVE

Revelation 2:4-5 Nevertheless I have somewhat against thee, because thou hast left thy first love. Remember therefore from whence thou art fallen, and repent, and do the first works; or else I will come unto thee quickly, and will remove thy candlestick out of his place, except thou repent.

The church at Ephesus was losing its zeal for the Lord. God reminded them to get back to it. Believers were slacking in some areas. God simply wants the church to repent and get back on track. The church's first love should be Jesus Christ! It means following Him and being obedient to Him and nothing outside of it.

I was just a young minister in 1998 when I met a gentleman working for the housing in Missouri on the military base. I asked him one question pertaining to God. The question was, "Do you know Jesus as your Lord and Savior?" I was asking this in the middle of him repairing my electrical wires in the house. He responded that he was once a pastor, but his wife left him for another man. He said that was enough to make him quit. It made me think about pastors having Jesus as their first love and the true call to ministry. So, it puzzled me to think that this once-upon-a-time pastor did not have Jesus any longer as his first love. He gave up on Jesus as being his Lord. It also made me realize that his wife was truly his lord. Some people are so committed to their marriage that they worship their spouse and not Jesus. I was hoping something would happen to spark something new inside of him to start serving Jesus again.

Every believer, whether they hold a ministry title or not, must make sure that Jesus is the first love in their lives. Almost everyone has had a first love in one way or another. We usually associate first love with a man and woman having a close, intimate relationship. Something has a hold on almost every person's hearts at an early age in high school or college. You don't have to try and remember who or what it was. For most women, a man who they thought they were in love with in the first relationship was considered their first love. The same applies to men who had a woman who he truly believed was the right one. She was your first love.

Jesus is the right one to set your heart on as the first love. Jesus will never be let down. No matter how bad things happen in your life, Jesus should still be your first love.

In this passage, the problem with the church of Ephesus is that people were losing their love for Jesus. Jesus tells them they need to repent and get back to their first love. It is easy to let something else try to take the place of the church and Jesus, as your Lord. Nevertheless, you need to stand your ground and tell the enemy that Jesus is the King of glory, King of Kings and Lord of Lords. Rebuke that enemy in Jesus' name. Tell your enemies that Jesus is the Alpha and Omega, the beginning and the end. Listen, no one is like Him in all existence. Tell everyone you know that Jesus is the lily of the valley and the bright and morning star! He can shine His light on my life. Jesus is the one you need honor, worship, praise and give thanksgiving to. Jesus is the Lord of your life!

If you have stopped attending church every Sunday, you are showing God that Jesus is not your first love. Get back into the church! Get back to doing the works of Jesus for the ministry and glorification of Jesus. Be a servant of Jesus Christ and do your first works over. Serve Him, worship Him, and praise Him. Witness His word of truth to others and glorify Him in all things. He wants to be priority. He wants to be your first love.

COLD OR HOT LOVE

Revelation 3:15-16 I know your works that you are neither cold nor hot, I could wish you were cold or hot. So then, because you are lukewarm, and neither cold nor hot, I will vomit you out of my mouth.

It seemed like a perfect day. We started discussing which season we prefer. I said that I love winter months. He said that he used to love hot seasons. Now he prefers it to be slightly warm. I thought about the effects and impact of a lukewarm person in God's Kingdom.

A lukewarm Christian will not do anything but attend church sometimes. God wants people on fire for Him! Jesus already knows our works. He knows if we are working because we love him or just going through the motions. How does He know it? He knows it because He is God. Nothing is hidden from Him. He knows we will be on fire in serving Him. He knows if we will ever witness and tell our children the goodness of God.

You should be on fire in your own house first! I work every day and at the end of the day, it dawns on me again that I must teach Bible study on Wednesday. Sometimes, it gets a quick thought to cancel it. However, the Holy Spirit reminds me that I can't cancel just because I'm tired after working all day. God gives me strength to teach and every Bible study turns out to be a blessing. I learn something every time.

One night, my wife sent me an email which said, "NO! You are not cancelling it." I was glad that I did not. I was able to continue with the fourth week in a row, talking about witnessing and pairing up teams. The title of the lesson was "Walking with God." This time, we had Bible study and more visitors arrived that had never been at Christian Worship Center. Everybody's involvement was great and it was a blessing! Then I gave them some exercises to have some fun.

During our study and illustrations, I realized one brother had an anointing on him. I could just tell by his confidence and answers. Later that day, I approached him. "Brother, are you a minister?" He hesitated before he responded, "Yes, Pastor." He went on to tell me his credentials. Nevertheless, it was powerful to me that God allowed me to discern his spirit. He was on fire and I could tell that he wanted more of the Holy Ghost. What's even more powerful is the fact that my wife was out witnessing and invited some students she knew, and this minister was one of them. You never know the entire story and what people do until you see their fruit because you planted!

My wife is powerful in her witnessing. She loves Jesus! This indicates clearly that they were hot and not lukewarm. A lukewarm person will hardly ever do anything for God and if they did, it is usually because of their pride and selfishness. God will do a work on them.

Cold and hot are two extremes in a positive direction in our witnessing for Jesus Christ. Lukewarm is not good! Lukewarm is that person that acts like he or she is not a follower of Jesus Christ. No one wants lukewarm water at any time. Lukewarm water is a turn off almost in every case. I want cold water to drink. I want hot water to wash my body and clean myself up with.

Lukewarm does not have the power to get positive results because it lacks effectiveness. Lukewarm, in my opinion, symbolizes stagnant, lazy, ineffectiveness and lack of love for Christ. However, when you're hot, you are on fire and moving fast for the almighty King of Glory. Remember John 15:1-12 If we are witnesses, we have an opportunity to be fruitful in God's Kingdom.

A TRUE CHRISTIAN ATHLETE

Philippians 3:10-14 that I may know Him and the power of His resurrection, and the fellowship of His sufferings, being conformed to His death, if, by any means, I may attain to the resurrection from the dead. Not that I have already attained, or am already perfected; but I press on, that I may lay hold of that for which Christ Jesus has also laid hold of me. Brethren, I do not count myself to have apprehended; but one thing I do, forgetting those things which are behind and reaching forward to those things which are ahead, I press toward the goal for the prize of the upward call of God in Christ Jesus.

There is a special passion and desire to be a professional athlete. Usually you'll know that sport inside out. There are also professional fans that spend their lifetime cheering their favorite team. This is a special announcement to those that have athletic talents and to their fans. God wants you to know Him better than you know sports.

Perhaps one of the roughest sports is football because the objective is to cross the goal line as many times as possible ending with the winning score. You must defeat the opposing team. Spiritually, the enemy (opposing team) is on your trail. God gave you the ability to be a professional athlete! Your skills will open doors to success and will give hope and encouragement to a large audience around the world on social media. Therefore, you can reach over 10 million people at the minimum by sharing the Word of God because of your famous status and talent.

Do you know God? This question is to every sports team on earth. There are a few football players who's been in the limelight to express their relationship with Jesus Christ. When are you going to witness? God placed upon my heart to encourage all athletes. The Lord is saying that it's time for every athlete to become effective witnesses for Jesus Christ. If you have an athletic talent or any other talent, God wants you to know that it came from Him! You received the blessing in that area because of God, not yourself! God had everything to do with your success! Therefore, the Lord wants you, as an athlete, to take on the attitude that the Apostle displays throughout the Bible. In Philippians 3:10-15, the Apostle Paul wanted us to know God and the power of His might who raised Jesus from the dead. He also reminds us to forget the past and press for the mark of prize of the high calling in Jesus Christ.

God only asked that you worship and praise His holy name. Yes, of course, having that talent is part of the favor from God; nevertheless, it's not the ultimate favor. The ultimate favor is having eternal life, knowing that you are born again in Jesus Christ. Because you've accepted Jesus, you've been justified. You have been redeemed. Acknowledge Jesus as your Lord, not the football, the basketball, the baseball or your Olympic gold medal.

The Bible says in *Philippians 2:10, "That at the name of Jesus every knee will bow, and every tongue will confess that Jesus is Lord in heaven, on earth and beneath the earth."* Those who reject Him because of their prideful millions, pretending that they are disciples, Jesus said in Matthew 7:21-23:

"Not everyone who says to me, 'Lord, Lord,' will enter the kingdom of heaven, but only the one who does the will of my Father who is in heaven. Many will say to me on that day, 'Lord, Lord, did we not prophesy in your name and in your name drive out demons and, in your name, perform many miracles?' Then I will tell them plainly, 'I never knew you. Away from me, you evildoers!"

Although they were covered in the blood and it covers their iniquity, they never served God or acknowledged Him as Lord and

Savior. They have never witnessed to other people that Jesus is the Lord of their life and that He has the power to forgive sin. I want to make sure that everyone understands that what you do for Jesus demonstrates if He is your Lord or if someone or something else is!

To each athlete, your life is supposed to be a witness to others in Jesus Christ. Can you imagine or fathom having helped to advance God's kingdom by winning at least one soul? But because of your status, you will win over five million people to turn their lives over to Jesus Christ (Romans 10:9) to be born again.

Most recently, I saw a swimmer named Michael Phelps who won 23 gold medals, three silver medal, and two bronze medals, totaling 28 medals in the swimming event during the World Olympic Games. Just this amazing accomplishment can set a fire in a person's heart to achieve their desire in sports, ministry or any ambition. We as Christians can win a heavenly crown if we are faithful and serve God as much as an Olympic gold medalist does in his event.

God also wants you to become a witness, sower and give back to Him your time, talent and seeds of faith. Be a witness and sower in God's kingdom to someone who needs a helping hand! You can do it in Jesus' name! You can become a true Christian that performs greater works in God's kingdom while giving Him the glory.

References

Bernstein, M. (2002). 10 tips on writing the living Web. *A List Apart: For People Who Make Websites, 149*. Retrieved from http://www.alistapart.com/articles/writeliving

Clarke, Adam. "Commentary on 1 Samuel 7:12". "The Adam Clarke Commentary". https:https://www.studylight.org/commentaries/acc/1-samuel-7.html. 1832.

Dobson E.G., Feinberg, C.L., Hindson, E.E. Kroll, W. M., & Wilmington H.L., (1994).Parallel Bible Commentary. *The complete King James Version*, p 2438.

ABOUT THE AUTHOR

Joseph Harris is the Senior Pastor and founder of Christian Worship Outreach Center Ministries. He has also served in military for several years and believes that soldiers are to be commended for their heroism. He also serves on the Board of Directors of Transforming Life Center to help AT- Risk Youth. He enjoys sports, productions and projects for uprising ministries. The most important things to Joseph is family and his passion to do the ministry that Jesus Christ has called him to do, (which is to witness and draw people to salvation). Pastor Harris is married and has children. He resides in Texas.

www.ingramcontent.com/pod-product-compliance
Lightning Source LLC
Chambersburg PA
CBHW022013160426
43197CB00007B/411